Addressing Compassion Fatigue in Urban Schools

As more students experience trauma and anxiety, the toll of teachers' compassion fatigue cannot be overlooked. This important book explores what compassion fatigue looks and feels like for teachers, who can become mentally and physically exhausted from caring and loving their students and may not want to stay in the profession as a result. Topics explore symptoms that may arise, the research on educator health and well-being, and strategies you can implement in your classroom and personal life to mitigate the effects. Each chapter offers vignettes to showcase teachers' experiences with compassion fatigue, reflection questions to help you relate to the content personally and professionally, and tools you can use throughout the school year. This powerful book equips teachers with the knowledge to make impactful decisions, enhancing their quality of life and improving school climate, working conditions, and the overall well-being of students.

Jacquelyn Ollison is an equity-focused education expert in improving teacher retention in high-poverty schools by addressing teachers' compassion fatigue. She is a featured TEDx speaker on educators' compassion fatigue, and she knows the impact compassion fatigue has on educators because it happened to her, and she left the classroom. She is the Director of the Center for Research on Expanding Educational Opportunity at UC Berkeley and an instructor at the UC Merced Extension Teacher Preparation Program.

Also Available from Routledge
Eye On Education
(www.routledge.com/K-12)

The Meditation and Mindfulness Edge: Becoming a Sharper, Healthier, and Happier Teacher
Lisa M. Klein

Mindfulness for Students: A Curriculum for Grades 3-8
Wendy Fuchs

Everyday Self-Care for Educators: Tools and Strategies for Well-Being
Carla Tantillo Philibert, Christopher Soto, Lara Veon

Embracing Adult SEL: An Educator's Guide to Personal Social Emotional Learning Success
Wendy Turner

Addressing Compassion Fatigue in Urban Schools
Strategies for Sowing Seeds of Resilience

Jacquelyn Ollison

NEW YORK AND LONDON

Designed cover image: © Getty Images

First published 2025
by Routledge
605 Third Avenue, New York, NY 10158

and by Routledge
4 Park Square, Milton Park, Abingdon, Oxon, OX14 4RN

Routledge is an imprint of the Taylor & Francis Group, an informa business

© 2025 Jacquelyn Ollison

The right of Jacquelyn Ollison to be identified as author of this work has been asserted in accordance with sections 77 and 78 of the Copyright, Designs and Patents Act 1988.

All rights reserved. No part of this book may be reprinted or reproduced or utilised in any form or by any electronic, mechanical, or other means, now known or hereafter invented, including photocopying and recording, or in any information storage or retrieval system, without permission in writing from the publishers.

Trademark notice: Product or corporate names may be trademarks or registered trademarks, and are used only for identification and explanation without intent to infringe.

Library of Congress Cataloging-in-Publication Data
Names: Ollison, Jacquelyn, author.
Title: Addressing compassion fatigue in urban schools: strategies for sowing seeds of resilience / Jacquelyn Ollison.
Description: New York, NY: Routledge, 2025. |
Series: Routledge eye on education | Includes bibliographical references.
Identifiers: LCCN 2024032580 (print) | LCCN 2024032581 (ebook) | ISBN 9781032537535 (hardback) | ISBN 9781032514277 (paperback) | ISBN 9781003413431 (ebook)
Subjects: LCSH: Teachers—Job stress—United States. | Secondary traumatic stress—United States. | Compassion—United States. | Teacher-student relationships—United States. | Education, Urban—United States—Social aspects.
Classification: LCC LB2840.2 .O55 2025 (print) | LCC LB2840.2 (ebook) | DDC 371.1001/9--dc23/eng/20240913
LC record available at https://lccn.loc.gov/2024032580
LC ebook record available at https://lccn.loc.gov/2024032581

ISBN: 978-1-032-53753-5 (hbk)
ISBN: 978-1-032-51427-7 (pbk)
ISBN: 978-1-003-41343-1 (ebk)

DOI: 10.4324/9781003413431

Typeset in Palatino
by codeMantra

Contents

About the Author vi
Preface: Can I Share Something with You? vii

1 The Slow Burn of Teaching: Understanding Compassion Fatigue in Urban School Teachers 1

2 Understanding Compassion Fatigue 24

3 Research Shows Teachers Suffer from Compassion Fatigue 50

4 Addressing Compassion Fatigue in Yourself 85

5 Sowing Seeds of Resilience 108

About the Author

Jacquelyn Ollison is an equity-focused education expert in improving teacher retention in high-poverty schools by addressing teachers' compassion fatigue. She is a featured TEDx speaker on educators' compassion fatigue, and she knows the impact compassion fatigue has on educators because it happened to her, and she left the classroom. She is the Director of the Center for Research on Expanding Educational Opportunity at UC Berkeley and an instructor at the UC Merced Extension Teacher Preparation Program.

Beyond her professional endeavors, Dr. Ollison contributes her voice and expertise to Safe Black Space (https://www.safeblackspace.org/) and the Torlakson Whole Child Institute as a board member, advocating for healing from racial trauma and holistic community solutions to educational challenges.

Her personal journey, marked by a transition from classroom teaching due to compassion fatigue, informs her advocacy for viewing educators as first responders, deserving of support and reverence. Dr. Ollison's insights on this topic have resonated with a wide audience through her publications and keynote speeches, including on the TEDx stage, which can be viewed at https://youtu.be/-Cmc-5sU5L4.

Residing in Northern California with her family and beloved dog Séo, Dr. Ollison continues to inspire change and foster environments where educators and students alike can thrive and achieve their fullest potential. Her pronouns are she/her/hers.

Preface:
Can I Share Something with You?

Dear Reader,

When I first studied compassion fatigue in 2019, I found statistically significant differences in compassion fatigue between teachers working at high-poverty schools and teachers working at low-poverty schools. Teachers at high-poverty schools tended to experience higher rates of burnout and secondary trauma. These rates were further exacerbated by student demographics such as ethnicity, English language learner status, and disability. Even more, female teachers experienced higher rates of compassion fatigue than their male counterparts. At the same time, the teacher shortage was seeing record highs. I knew then that if something was not done, the teaching profession was headed for a dark period worse than we had seen. In California alone, about 73% of the teaching population is female, over 60% of the student population is considered socioeconomically disadvantaged, and about 20% are English Learners – compassion fatigue is a genuine concern for teachers. And it is only going to get worse if we do not address it.

In its simplest form, compassion fatigue is the "natural consequent behaviors and emotions resulting from knowing about a traumatizing event experienced by a significant other – the stress resulting from helping or wanting to help a traumatized or suffering person" (Figley, 1995, p.8). The cumulative effects of the use of empathy, combined with secondary traumatic stress (STS) and burnout, can lead to a generalized syndrome known as Compassion Fatigue (Figley, 1995; Newell & MacNeil, 2010). Stamm (2010) conceptualizes Compassion Fatigue as the combination of secondary trauma and burnout. Burnout causes "feelings of hopelessness and difficulties in dealing with work or in doing your job effectively" (p. 13), while STS is "about work-related, secondary exposure to people who have experienced extremely or traumatically stressful events" (p. 13). Both of which have negative consequences for the helping professional. Though they share common symptoms, what makes compassion fatigue different is that one must be dealing with a traumatized population to develop it (Lerias & Byrne, 2003). Left unaddressed, compassion fatigue can be problematic for practitioners charged with the care and support of those suffering from trauma (Figley, 1995) (Ollison, 2019a, p. 152).

Individuals suffering from compassion fatigue may experience adverse mental health effects like depression, physical, mental, and emotional exhaustion, irritability, chronic illness, apathy, anxiety, and a decreased ability to feel empathy and compassion for others. Moreover, a system suffering from compassion fatigue may experience chronic absenteeism, high turnover rates, and friction between staff and management (Ollison, 2019a). Unfortunately, all these symptoms are present in our teacher workforce. "As long as students are experiencing trauma, and teachers provide mental, emotional, and physical support in response to it – teachers are…working with trauma victims. And experiencing trauma, sometimes firsthand but mostly second-hand, on a daily basis" (Ollison, 2019b). They deserve our respect, care, attention, and support, but they are not getting it in the ways that matter. For example, teachers are left out of support offered to traditional first responders (*First Responder Support Network*, n.d.). And efforts to get them proper training like mental health first aid fall on deaf ears (*California SB428 | 2019-2020 | Regular Session*, n.d.). Even though, like police, firefighters, social workers, therapists, and medical personnel, teachers respond to school emergencies.

The 2012 Sandy Hook school shooting is an example of this, where 20 first-graders and 6 teachers were murdered or the 2022 Robb Elementary School Shooting in Uvalde, Texas, where 19 students and 2 teachers were killed (Brumfield, 2012; Ulloa et al., 2022). Those teachers protected those kids with their lives, and in the aftermath, they were there to pick up the pieces in the form of mental, emotional, and physical support. They also respond to natural disasters like the wildfires and mudslides in California, such as the Camp Fire, which destroyed 14,000 homes and displaced 32,000 kids from school (Anguiano, 2021). Those students eventually returned, ensuring that teachers would be dealing with the aftermath of that trauma in classrooms and school campuses for years to come.

And teachers once again rose to the occasion as they responded to the student trauma caused by the COVID-19 pandemic. Like many of us, students lost close loved ones due to COVID (Jones, 2021). They have also dealt with their parents lost jobs and wages, homelessness, increased violence, and the loss of their social network due to school closures; their mental health has suffered as a result. For students of color, the disproportionate impact has left many orphaned due to significantly higher death rates in the Black, Latinx, and Pacific Islander communities (Department of Public Health, n.d.).

Supporting students' grief is a lot for anyone to take on, yet teachers do. When children are experiencing trauma, the resulting behavior is not always pleasant, ranging from sullen behavior to apathy and problematic outbursts (NCTSN, n.d.). Imagine trying to recognize the signs of trauma to support students' health and well-being or respond to an emergency while teaching the subject matter you are credentialed in without proper mental health and emergency response training. It would be difficult, right? Yet, teachers do this daily, and that is the problem.

James Baldwin said, "Not everything that is faced can be changed, but nothing can be changed until it is faced" (Baldwin, 1962). We have yet to face the fact that first responder teachers are suffering from compassion fatigue – or the physical, mental, and emotional exhaustion that comes from working with people in constant distress (Lerias & Byrne, 2003), the combination of burnout and secondary traumatic stress (Stamm, 2010). First responders who work with child trauma victims are more susceptible to compassion fatigue (Ollison, 2019a).

The teacher shortage, which existed well before the pandemic, has worsened, with 77% of district leaders showing moderate to severe staffing shortages (Lieberman, 2021). Thankfully, much research has been done to address the complex reasons for teacher shortages, such as improving working conditions, creating supportive and positive school climates, increasing compensation, and addressing recruitment and retention simultaneously with grow-your-own programs like teacher residencies (Kini, 2022). There has also been an increase in the call for trauma-informed mental health support for students and teachers (Coles et al., 2022). However, more is needed because none of them seriously address educator's compassion fatigue.

The collective recognition of the teaching staffing shortage and the trauma caused by the pandemic is a sign that we are now ready to see and address compassion fatigue in teachers as an important enough policy issue (Ollison, 2019a). In 2019, I argued that if California is "serious about producing and retaining high-quality teachers at all schools, particularly at urban schools, efforts to mitigate Compassion Fatigue should be undertaken immediately" (p. 208). It is now 2024, and I am making this same plea again. I recently conducted a study to see how the pandemic affected teachers' experience with compassion fatigue and found that now there is no statistically significant difference in compassion fatigue rates between a teacher at high- and low-poverty schools. Burnout rates and secondary trauma rates are high across the board. In other words, we are in trouble.

In the pages that follow, we will explore research about compassion fatigue and the teaching profession and how compassion fatigue impacts teachers' perception of their school climate and working conditions in relation to teacher shortages and retention challenges. Specifically, we will learn what compassion fatigue looks and feels like for teachers, symptoms that may arise, and strategies, tools, and recommendations to support their health and well-being. It is my hope that you will be armed with enough awareness and knowledge to make powerful choices that improve the professional quality of life of teachers and, by extension, school climate and working conditions, and ultimately the social, emotional, and academic well-being of all students.

Working with the added stress that compassion fatigue brings is unhealthy for teachers and the students they serve; the cost is too high. This is why attending to teachers' physical, mental, and emotional well-being is now more critical than ever (Ollison, 2019a). Happy reading.

Respectfully,
Dr. J
Jacquelyn Ollison, Ed.D.

References

Anguiano, D. (2021, October 22). California: 32,000 kids return to class on Monday after wildfires hit schools. *California | The Guardian*. Retrieved June 17, 2024, from https://amp.theguardian.com/us-news/2018/nov/30/california-wildfires-schools-paradise

Baldwin, J. (1962, January 14). AS MUCH TRUTH AS ONE CAN BEAR; To Speak Out About the World as It Is, Says James Baldwin, Is the Writer's Job As Much of the Truth as One Can Bear. *The New York Times*. https://www.nytimes.com/1962/01/14/archives/as-much-truth-as-one-can-bear-to-speak-out-about-the-world-as-it-is.html?auth=login-google1tap&login=google1tap

Brumfield, B. (2012, December 18). Connecticut teachers were heroes in the face of death. *CNN*. Retrieved November 26, 2023, from https://www.cnn.com/2012/12/17/us/connecticut-shooting-teacher-heroism

California SB428 | 2019-2020 | Regular Session: SB-428 Pupil Health: School employee training: youth mental and behavioral health. (n.d.). LegiScan. Retrieved June 17, 2024, from https://legiscan.com/CA/bill/SB428/2019

Coles, D., Manassah, T., & Schwerner, C. (2022, April 7). Mental health crises are bombarding our schools. Here's what we can do (Opinion). *Education Week*. Retrieved June 17, 2024, from https://www.edweek.org/leadership/opinion-mental-health-crises-are-bombarding-our-schools-heres-what-we-can-do/2022/03

Department of Public Health. (n.d.). *COVID-19 home*. Retrieved June 17, 2024, from https://covid19.ca.gov/smarter

Figley, Charles R. (1995) Compassion fatigue as secondary traumatic stress disorder: An overview. *Compassion Fatigue: Coping with secondary traumatic stress disorder in those who treat the traumatized (Psychosocial Stress Series), 1*, 1–18. Taylor and Francis. Kindle Edition.

First Responder Support Network. (n.d.). First Responder Support Network. Retrieved June 17, 2024, from https://www.frsn.org/

Jones, C. (2021, August 13). How schools help students who've lost loved ones to Covid. *EdSource*. Retrieved June 17, 2024, from https://edsource.org/2021/how-schools-help-students-whove-lost-loved-ones-to-covid/659527?amp=1

Kini, T. (2022, January 11). *Tackling teacher shortages: What can states and districts do?* Learning Policy Institute Solving Teacher Shortages. Retrieved June 17, 2024, from https://learningpolicyinstitute.org/blog/teacher-shortage-what-can-states-and-districts-do

Lerias, D., & Byrne, M. K. (2003). Vicarious traumatization: Symptoms and predictors. *Stress and Health*, *19*(3), 129–138. https://doi.org/10.1002/smi.969

Lieberman, M. (2021, October 22). How bad are school staffing shortages? What we learned by asking administrators. *Education Week*. Retrieved June 17, 2024, from https://www.edweek.org/leadership/how-bad-are-school-staffing-shortages-what-we-learned-by-asking-administrators/2021/10

Ollison, J. (2019a, June). *Improving teacher retention by addressing teachers' compassion fatigue*. Scholarly Commons. Retrieved June 17, 2024, from https://scholarlycommons.pacific.edu/uop_etds/3602/

Ollison, J. (2019b, November 13). *Compassion Fatigue | Jacquelyn Ollison | TEDxOhloneCollege* [Video]. YouTube - TEDx Talks. Retrieved from https://www.youtube.com/watch?v=-Cmc-5sU5L4

Newell, J. M., & MacNeil, G. A. (2010). Professional burnout, vicarious trauma, secondary traumatic stress, and compassion fatigue: A review of theoretical terms, risk factors, and preventive methods for clinicians and researchers. *Best Practices in Mental Health*, *6*(2), 57–68.

Stamm, B. H. (2010) *The Concise ProQOL Manual* (2nd ed.). Pocatello, ID: ProQOL.org.

The National Child Traumatic Stress Network. (n.d.). The National Child Traumatic Stress Network (NCTSN). Retrieved June 17, 2024, from https://www.nctsn.org/resources/addressing-race-and-trauma-classroom-resource-teachers

Ulloa, J., Goodman, J. D., Bogel-Burroughs, N., & Bosman, J. (2022, May 25). Uvalde elementary school shooting: Families in Texas grieve loss of 19 children in shooting. *New York Times*. Retrieved June 17, 2024, from https://www.nytimes.com/live/2022/05/25/us/shooting-robb-elementary-uvalde. Updated June 2, 2022

1

The Slow Burn of Teaching: Understanding Compassion Fatigue in Urban School Teachers

Urban teachers face a unique set of challenges that go beyond the classroom walls. Central to understanding these challenges is the concept of "compassion fatigue," an emotional and psychological exhaustion that emerges from the constant demand and struggle to address the traumatic experiences of students (Ollison, 2019a). This chapter delves into how compassion fatigue contributes to high attrition rates among teachers in urban school settings, underscoring the need for systemic change.

Teacher Resiliency Is Not Enough

Teachers who work in inner-city urban schools have a calling (Brunetti, 2006). They work at these types of schools because they are aware of the impact their presence can have on urban students. Teachers at inner-city urban schools are often dedicated to making a difference in the lives of their students. They understand that the educational gaps between urban students and their peers can be closed by providing extra support, resources, effective instruction, and care. They also recognize the potential of these schools to contribute to the development of a strong urban community.

> **Pause and Reflect:** *Why did you become a teacher?*

Urban teachers are resilient; even when facing the challenges of teaching students experiencing troubling circumstances, they remain in the profession at urban school sites because it is where they feel they belong (Brunetti, 2006). At the same time, unpleasant working conditions such as high job demands and low pay can lead to teacher burnout (Mathews & Hart Research Associates, 2022). Together, these circumstances are taking their toll on teachers, and despite their resilience, teachers are leaving urban schools in droves (Brown & Wynn, 2009). This leads to one of the most significant barriers urban students face: a pervasive teacher shortage (Sutcher et al., 2018). In the absence of quality teachers, school districts are resorting to troubling methods to fill vacancies. Research shows that school districts are "hiring substitutes at high rates (24%), assigning teachers to positions outside of their credential field (22%), leaving positions vacant (17%), increasing class sizes (9%), and canceling courses (8%)" (LPI, 2017). What's more, 71% of high-poverty districts hire teachers with substandard credentials, and 29% hire substitutes to teach core academics such as Mathematics and English Language Arts (Podolsky et al., 2016).

As a result of this teacher shortage urban students are receiving sub-par education reflected in persistent, pervasive, and widening achievement and opportunity gaps (Carver-Thomas et al., 2020; EdTrust-West, 2015). For example, in California African American and Hispanic students score 10–30 percentage points lower than their White and Asian counterparts. Additionally, urban students are usually the first to be suspended and taught by ineffective teachers (George & Darling-Hammond, 2019; EdTrust-West, 2015). This gap is not urban students' fault. Systemic social inequities are barriers urban students face that make successful education attainment difficult, if not impossible, (APA Task Force on Urban Psychology, 2005; Reardon & Bischoff, 2011). Let's look at why.

Secondary Trauma Impedes Teacher Self-Efficacy

Alice, Elementary School Teacher

My students come from diverse backgrounds, and they have different personalities and behavior issues. I think it is easier to handle students' issues when you are dealing with four and five-year-old students. Though easy may not be the right word. I think I am more accepting of it because they are so young. Because, as a teacher, you deal with a whole lot of emotion. I try really hard not to bring my personal situations into the classroom so that I can deal with my students' personal situation because my classroom is a safe haven; but, emotionally it's a bit much. You know, when I first became a teacher, sometimes I would come home and cry just seeing the situation that these kids have to deal with, and not knowing what they're going to go back home to when they leave my classroom. It hurt my heart actually. It was a bit emotional. I did have some sleepless nights worrying about what was going to happen to this child or the well-being of that child. There were days where I didn't want to be in the classroom. There were days I would have to deal with myself and deal with pulling my emotions together. At times it did affect me and my teaching abilities. Eventually, I decided that I couldn't give my students all my worrying about a specific situation or something like that. I had to pull myself together and I told myself, 'it's not about me, it's about these kids, and you are all they have right now in this classroom. I have to be stronger than this, even though it did bother me.'

Vignette Originally Appeared in (Ollison, 2019a, pg. 129).

 Pause and Reflect: *Do you agree with what Alice shared in the vignette? Why or why not?*

Why Urban Schools Look the Way They Do

The socioeconomic and racial demographics of urban schools, which typically have a majority of students of color or high-poverty students, didn't just occur naturally; they were created by public policy (Aliprantis, 2023; Rothstein, 2017).

> Today's residential segregation in the North, South, Midwest, and West is not the unintended consequence of individual choices and of otherwise well-meaning law or regulation but of unhidden public policy that explicitly segregated every metropolitan area in the United States.
> (Rothstein, 2017, location 52)

In 1934, under President Roosevelt, The Federal Housing Administration (FHA) as part of the National Housing Act meant to combat the loss of many homes due to the great depression was established (Rothstein, 2017). The FHA helped to stimulate the mortgage economy by insuring mortgage loans for home ownership, commercial and rental property, and property repairs. In doing so, it helped lower interest rates, lengthen the amount of time people had to repay the loans, and improve neighborhoods and the mortgage market (National Housing Agency, 1946). As part of this effort the FHA developed an underwriting manual to provide instructions regarding how to insure mortgage loans and to assess the risk of borrowers (FHA, 1938). Section nine of this manual included explicit instructions designed to "determine the degree of mortgage risk involved because of the location of a property at a specific site" (FHA, 1938, Paragraph 906). This 100-point location rating system was based on eight categories, summarized in more detail in FHA (1938) Paragraph 987. I have summarized an excerpt of section from the *FHA Underwriting Manual: Underwriting And Valuation Procedure Under Title II Of The National Housing Act* for you in Table 1.1. The complete text can be found and downloaded for free at https://www.huduser.gov/portal/sites/default/files/pdf/Federal-Housing-Administration-Underwriting-Manual.pdf.

TABLE 1.1 Summary of Each Feature of Mortgage Risk Rating by Location

Relative Economic Stability (40 points)
- Stability of Family Incomes
- Sufficiency of Family Incomes
- Social Characteristics of Neighborhood Occupants
- Stage and Trend of Neighborhood Development
- Probability of Forced Sales and Foreclosures

Protection from Adverse Influences (20 points)
- Zoning
- Restrictive Covenants
- Natural Physical Protection
- Surrounding Homogeneous Neighborhood
- Quality of Neighboring Development
- Ribbon Developments
- Nuisances

Freedom from Special Hazards (5 points)
- Topography
- Subsidence
- Earthquake, Tornado, or Hurricane Hazard
- Flood Hazard
- Traffic Hazard
- Fire and Explosion Hazards
- Hazards to Health

Adequacy of Civic, Social, and Commercial Centers (5 points)
- Quality and Accessibility of Schools
- Quality and Accessibility of Shopping Centers and Amusements
- Quality and Accessibility of Churches, Clubs, and Recreation Centers

Sufficiency of Utilities and Conveniences (5 points)
- Presence of Required Utilities
- Quality of Utilities
- Cost of Services

Level of Taxes and Special Assessments (5 points)
- Relationship of Tax Burden with Competitive Locations
- Nature, Cost, and Duration of Special Assessments

Appeal (10 points)
- Natural Physical Charm and Beauty of Location
- Geographical Position of Location
- Layout and Plan of Neighborhood
- Architectural Attractiveness of Buildings
- Social Attractiveness
- Nuisances

Each of these categories had criteria that needed to be assessed and included in the ratings total. Given the time period and the countries attitudes toward racial groups at the time, you can see that this system was designed to ensure that home ownership and thriving neighborhoods were reserved for the White families or for builders who would build and sell to White families. African Americans and other people of color were not generally wealthy and thus would not rate high in the *Relative Economic Stability* category.

The *Protection from Adverse Influences* was the second highest rated category and thus very important. This category detailed how public policy backed zoning ordinances could be used to keep out adverse influences. Specifically, it says:

> If the provisions of an ordinance have been well worded and drawn from a thorough knowledge of existing and probable future conditions in the city, and if the ordinance receives the backing of public approval, an excellent basis for protection from adverse influences exists. If an ordinance has been drawn with little or no real understanding of its purpose, or without a desire to promote an orderly city growth, or if it lacks public approval, the chances are that it will offer little protection from adverse influences
>
> (FHA, 1938, Paragraph 933)

It also argues that zoning ordinances may not be enough and thus restrictive covenants "where the restrictions relate to types of structures, use to which improvements may be put, and occupancy," to keep out adverse influences must also be used and enforced (FHA, 1938, Paragraph 934).

The geographical position of a location is also described as a way to provide reliable protection from adverse influences. Geographically desired locations include locations in the middle of an area well developed with a uniform type of residential properties because they will likely be immune to change in type, use, or occupancy. Likewise, locations with natural and artificial barriers like public parks, hills, ravines, high-speed traffic arteries, and wide street parkways are desirable. The locations should not have high-speed traffic arteries passing directly through it. They also cannot be close to railroads, elevated or surface lines, and other means of transportation because this could facilitate infiltration of adverse influences rather than protection. Specifically, it states, "Usually the protection from adverse influences afforded by these means includes prevention of the infiltration of business and industrial uses, lower class occupancy, and inharmonious racial groups" (FHA, 1938, Paragraph 935).

This category also describes the quality of the neighboring development as needing to be well constructed, free from large amounts of old homes, lacking under or over improvements, and that the:

> Areas surrounding a location are investigated to determine whether incompatible racial and social groups are present, for the purpose of making a prediction regarding the probability of the location being invaded by such groups. If a neighborhood is to retain stability, it is necessary that properties shall continue to be occupied by the same social and racial classes. A change in social or racial occupancy generally contributes to instability and a decline in values.
>
> (FHA, 1938, Paragraph 937)

The rating location system also helped ensure that approved mortgages were for homes that were free of hazards that could endanger the safety or health of occupants. Meaning that the homes weren't built in flood zones, earthquake zones, fire or explosion zones, heavy traffic areas, or other negative conditions like "smoke, fog, chemical fumes, exhaust gases, stagnant ponds or marshes, poor surface drainage, and excessive heat or dampness" (FHA, 1938, Paragraph 948).

This system also explains that for a neighborhood to remain stable and retain desirability, it must be adequately served by grade and high schools, neighborhood shopping centers, churches, theaters, parks, playgrounds, community halls, libraries, and colleges (FHA, 1938, Paragraph 949). The quality of the schools in the neighborhood was a huge consideration in risk assessment. Social class of the families in the neighborhood mattered as well as whether or not

> the children of people living in such an area are compelled to attend school where the majority or a considerable number of the pupils represent a far lower level of society or an incompatible racial element, the neighborhood under consideration will prove far less stable and desirable than if this condition did not exist.
> (FHA, 1938, Paragraph 951)

Separate but equal was the law of the land, but this powerful policy clearly outlines how unequal our country was and, in many ways, still is (Rothstein, 2017). This policy led to redlining in which neighborhoods were color-coded red if mostly people of color lived in them. The inhabitants of red neighborhoods were not given loans by financial institutions to purchase homes in suburban areas, while their White counterparts did receive loans, which had the effect of keeping neighborhoods segregated and unequal (APA Task Force on Urban Psychology, 2005; L. Darling-Hammond & S. Darling-Hammond, 2024; Florida, 2017; NPR 2017; Rothstein 2017).

 Pause and Reflect: *Do you notice a difference in the quality of neighborhoods between the high-poverty and low-poverty schools in your school district?*

Rothstein (2017) explains that this "segregation by intentional government action is not de facto. Rather, it is what courts call de jure: segregation by law and public policy" (location 52). Although the information presented here was written in 1938 it has had a multigenerational impact on the wealth, health, and schooling of every generation of people since. This impact continues today even with the passage of the 1968 Fair Housing Act designed to end racial discriminatory housing practices of sales and rentals based on race, religion, or nationality (Schill & Friedman, 1998). According to The Civil Rights Project, "Black, Latino, and Native students [marginalized student populations] are more likely to be poor and far more likely to live and go to school in areas of concentrated poverty because of the combined force of economic barriers and discrimination" (Orfield & Pfleger, 2024, p. 43). In 2021, the United States threshold rates for poverty were defined as individuals with incomes below $12,880 and households with incomes below $26,500 for a family of four (Poverty - Healthy People 2030 | *Health.gov*, n.d.). The percentage of poor students in schools is defined as the number of students who qualify for free and reduced priced meals (NCES, 2023).

As of 2021, "the average Latino student attended a school that had 60.7% poor students and the average Black student attended a school with 60.5% poor students. The average Asian and White students attended schools with 36.9% and 35.1% students in poverty" (Orfield & Pfleger, 2024, p. 44). What's more, "Black and Latino students were the most highly segregated in 2021. Though U.S. schools were 45% white, Blacks, on average, attended 76% nonwhite schools, Latino students 75% nonwhite" (Orfield & Pfleger, 2024, p. 4). These marginalized populations of students attend double-segregated schools by income level and race (Orfield & Pfleger, 2024). Government-sanctioned public policies such as the *mortgage underwriting policy* described here have shaped the conditions in which urban students learn and educators are now working (APA Task Force on Urban Psychology, 2005; Florida, 2017; NPR 2017; Rothstein, 2017).

The Impact of Poverty on Urban Students Physical and Mental Health

Now that you understand why urban schools tend to have large populations of high-poverty marginalized students of color. Research also shows that children living in poverty likely means they have limited access to resources needed to support a healthy quality of life, including stable housing, healthy foods, affordable health care, safe neighborhoods, and thriving schools (L. Darling-Hammond & S. Darling-Hammond, 2024). Across their lifetimes, students living in poverty are at increased risk for experiencing violence, high rates of crime, overpopulated environments, scarce resources, mental illness, chronic disease, higher mortality, lower life expectancy, developmental delays, toxic stress, chronic illness, nutritional deficits, and lack of access to adequate health care and healthy food (Rothstein, 2017).

What's more, these risks also contribute to the low achievement of high-poverty students of color because of the impact on students' health, which may include "lack of access to eyeglasses, disproportionate instances of lead poisoning, iron-deficiency anemia, asthma, and substandard pediatric care" (L. Darling-Hammond & S. Darling-Hammond, 2024, p. 9). They may also experience perpetuated generational cycles of poverty, with children who experience poverty more likely to continue experiencing it as adults (Osofsky et al, 1993; Poverty - Healthy People 2030 | *Health.gov*, n.d.; Rothstein, 2017).

Tragically, urban students are also more likely to experience violence and homelessness that affects their physical and mental health (APA Task Force on Urban Psychology, 2005; Berman, 1996; Hart et al., 2012; Jiang et al., 2014). And after COVID, all students experienced profound impacts to their physical, social, emotional, mental health, and well-being (NEA, 2022). Exposure to disproportionate amounts of violence – whether victim or witness – can lead urban children to experience mental and psychological health issues such as post-traumatic stress disorder (PTSD). For instance, children exposed to higher levels of violence are more likely to suffer from depression, anxiety, and difficulty sleeping (*Children Exposed to Violence | National Institute of Justice*, 2016).

At this point you might be thinking why you should care, but here is why. Put simply, urban students experience trauma (APA Task Force on Urban Psychology, 2005). It is imperative that educators working with urban students understand this and receive support to effectively teach them. "Many traumatized children adopt behavioral coping mechanisms that can frustrate educators and evoke exasperated reprisals" (Cole et al., 2005, p. 32), which is evidence that student trauma enters the school system and manifests as issues educators must juggle alongside their many other professional tasks (Abraham-Cook, 2012; Hill, 2010). It can be challenging physically, emotionally, and mentally, especially if educators are not trained to recognize signs of trauma in students, such as difficulty concentrating, hyperactivity, and difficulty paying attention.

Research shows that PTSD is often an urban student condition where PTSD is defined as "an anxiety disorder that can occur following the experience or witnessing of a traumatic event" (Osofsky et al., 1993; Post-Traumatic Stress Disorder, n.d.; Schwartz et al., 2005; Thompson & Massat, 2005). Symptoms of PTSD in urban students can manifest as poor behavior including withdrawal, exaggerated startle responses, rudeness, irritability, truancy, risky sexual behavior, drug and alcohol abuse, classroom misbehavior, and academic difficulties (APA Task Force on Urban Psychology, 2005; Reynolds et al., 2001; Breslau et al., 1999). Educators are struggling to manage these traumas that expressed behaviors with skill and care because they have not been explicitly taught how to do so. Teachers must be prepared to provide appropriate support, such as recognizing when students are having a trauma response so that they can make referrals to mental health professionals, to help students cope with trauma. Teachers should also be prepared to handle the potential but probable impact of students' trauma on their own professional and mental health. It's only fair. But do you ever wonder why this issue has not been definitely addressed in ways that matter for you or all teachers everywhere? Read on to find out why.

The Nature of the School System

The educational system has created conditions that make it easy for teachers to become overwhelmed by issues of burnout and student trauma. Let's explore why. In Figure 1.1, you see an adapted conceptualized model of a school system based on California (Ollison, 2019a).

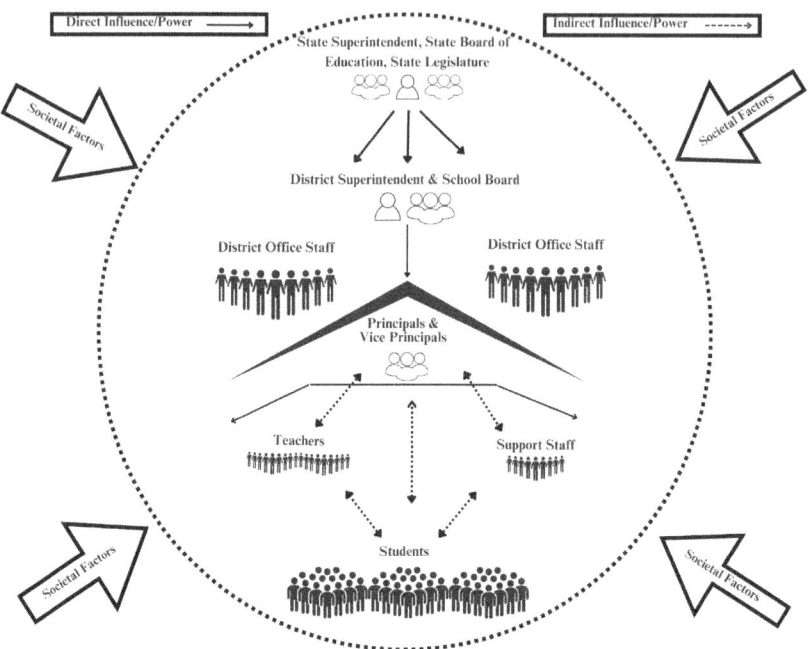

FIGURE 1.1 Adapted Conceptual School System Model (Ollison, 2019a)

At the top of the hierarchy is the State Superintendent of Public Instruction, State Board of Education, and State Legislature, who make decisions about the direction of education for the state. They also adopt rules and regulations, and pass bills, respectively, that influence the work of all school districts statewide. At the local level, the top decision-makers are the Superintendent and School Board comprised of elected officials (Meador, 2018), who make decisions about the overall vision, mission, and direction of the school district with the intent of ensuring that those within the system have what they need to do the work (Mintzberg, 1979). This direction is then translated and operationalized by administrators (e.g., Principals and Vice-Principals) who encourage and support the teachers and school support staff to implement the organizational direction successfully. Teachers are professionals who work autonomously within their classrooms to teach students despite common connections such as curriculum standards and shared groups of students (1979). But the hierarchical layers of the system can disrupt communication flows, often preventing teachers' needs from reaching the leadership at the top resulting in a lack of systemic coherence (Fullan & Quinn, 2016; Salancik & Pfeffer, 1977).

Drawing on organizational structure theory to view schools from a macro-perspective, we can see that the bureaucratic nature of the school system is such that school leaders and those influencing and making policy decisions such as politicians in the legislature are often far removed from the teacher experience due to the hierarchical nature of the system (Kirtman & Fullan, 2016; Mintzberg, 1979).

School Administrators Do Not Always Understand Teacher's Everyday Classroom Experience

Alex, Middle School Teacher

You know just once I wish my administration would acknowledge how difficult it is to teach at a high poverty, urban school. The kid's home lives are tough, you know. A lot of the students are experiencing some really horrific circumstances. Then when I try to teach them, just getting them to care is a chore in itself. And then their behavior, oh my gosh, it can be over the top. It takes its toll on me. So just once, just once, I would like it to be acknowledged that working at this school is harder than other schools. That alone would go a long way in letting me know that my administration sees me and understands what I am dealing with on a daily basis.

Vignette Originally Appeared in (Ollison, 2019a, p. 131).

 Pause and Reflect: *Do you agree with what Alex shared in the vignette? Why or why not?*

The Problem with the School Systems Nature

I believe the system design both creates and perpetuates trauma conditions for both urban students and their teachers. The school system does not see that teachers are leaving the school system in droves due to teachers' proximity to student trauma, and the toll secondary trauma has on teachers' perceptions of their school working conditions and climate. What's more,

> as long as students are experiencing trauma, and teachers provide mental, emotional, and physical support in response to it – teachers are in effect working with trauma victims. And, experiencing trauma, sometimes firsthand but mostly second hand, on a daily basis.
> (Ollison, 2019b)

Teachers deserve our respect, care, attention, and support, but they are not getting it in the ways that matter.

In a sense, all *teachers are first responders too*. Like the police, firefighters, social workers, therapists, and medical personnel, teachers respond to emergencies in schools like the Sandy Hook shooting, where 20 first-graders and 6 educators were murdered (Brumfield, 2012). Those educators protected those kids with their lives, and in the aftermath, they were there to pick up the pieces in the form of mental, emotional, and physical support. They also respond to natural disasters like wildfires and mudslides in such as the California Camp Fire, which destroyed 14,000 homes and displaced 32,000 kids from school (Anguiano, 2021). Those students eventually returned ensuring that teachers would deal with the aftermath of that trauma in classrooms and school campuses for years to come. And teachers are on the front lines as they continue to deal with the aftermath of students' trauma experience caused by the COVID-19 pandemic.

Like many of us, students have lost close loved ones due to COVID (Jones, 2021). They have also dealt with their parents' lost jobs and wages, homelessness, and the loss of their social network due to school closures. And their mental health has suffered as a result. For students of color, the disproportionate impact left many orphaned due to significantly higher COVID-19 death rates in the Black, Latinx, and Pacific Islander communities (California, n.d.).

Supporting students' trauma and grief is a lot for anyone to take on, and yet teachers do. When children experience trauma, the resulting behavior is not always pleasant, ranging from sullen behavior to apathy and problematic outbursts (Nctsnadmin, 2018). Imagine trying to recognize the signs of trauma to support a student's health and well-being, all while teaching the subject matter you are credentialed in without proper mental health training. It would be difficult, right? Yet teachers do this every day, without proper training and support, and that is the problem.

 Pause and Reflect: *Do you agree that teachers are first responders? Why or why not?*

In 1962, renowned author James Baldwin said, "Not everything that is faced can be changed, but nothing can be changed until it is faced." We have yet to face the fact that first responder teachers are suffering from compassion fatigue – the combination of burnout and secondary traumatic stress (Stamm, 2010). What's more, first responders who work with child trauma victims are more susceptible to compassion fatigue (Ollison, 2019a). In the next chapter we will delve more deeply into compassion fatigue exploring what it is, symptoms, factors of susceptibility, but for now it is enough to say that it is a problem that has been linked to teacher attrition (Ollison, 2019a).

Thankfully, much research and work has been done to address the complex reasons for teacher shortages. These include improving working conditions, creating supportive and positive school climates, increasing compensation, and addressing recruitment and retention simultaneously with grow-your-own programs like teacher residencies (Coles et al., 2022). There has even been an increase in the call for trauma-informed mental health support for students and educators (Coles et al., 2022). However, more is needed because none of them seriously address educator's compassion fatigue. I am hopeful that the collective recognition of the teaching staffing shortage and the trauma caused by the COVID-19 pandemic is a sign that compassion fatigue in educators is a significant enough policy issue to address with individual and collective action (Walker, 2023; Ollison, 2019a).

Tool 1.1 – It Starts with Why

Description: A tool to help you remember why you chose to enter the teaching profession.

Overview: Part of understanding our own healing journey as an educator starts with respecting both our student's humanity and our own. Yet, this respect can fall by the wayside under stressful conditions. Michael Jr. (2017) said in a video on YouTube, "When you know your why, your what becomes more impactful because you're walking towards or in your purpose." As teachers, remembering your why can help ground your teaching career in purpose and meaning.

Directions:

1. Watch the YouTube video "Know your why" by Michael Jr. at https://www.youtube.com/watch?v=1ytFB8TrkTo.
2. Then spend a few moments engaging in deep breathing.
3. Then close your eyes and reflect on this question: why did you want to be a teacher?
4. Write a one-two paragraph response on why you chose the teaching profession.
5. Next, write down three to five words that capture your why.
6. Place those words on a small notepaper and place them somewhere where you will see it every day (e.g., on your mirror, in your desk, in your wallet).
7. Look at them every time you need a boost of energy to face a day of teaching move with as much grace and compassion as you can muster.

Example: My why is simple and it informs all my decisions. Education gave me the skills to make life choices that support my dreams. I want to make sure that I am sowing seeds of light (e.g., knowledge, support, care) so that children, young and old, will grow and manifest their dreams. As I remember this, it gives me the boost of energy needed to push through to the next day and to thrive even in the most harrowing of conditions. *Education is Sacred Work*

Unfortunately, the school system is set up so that the conditions leading to teacher compassion fatigue are not readily seen nor understood. In this way, it will be difficult to enact systemwide policies to address compassion fatigue in teachers fast enough to make a difference for you in this moment. This is why addressing teacher's compassion fatigue must start with you. Given the interconnectedness of the parts of the school system and the influence system actors have on one another, any action you take to address it will not only make a difference for you it, but it will also impact the school system and lead to improvement in the school climate and well-being for staff and students alike (Boell & Senge, 2016; Fullan & Quinn, 2015).

 Connect the Thoughts

1. What insights/feelings does reading this chapter evoke in you?
2. Do you believe educators or first responders? Why or why not?
3. Describe your reaction to reading FHA (1938) Section 987?
4. What did you learn in this chapter that surprised you?

References

Abraham-Cook, S. (2012). The Prevalence and Correlates of Compassion Fatigue, Compassion Satisfaction, and Burnout among Teachers Working in High-Poverty Urban Public Schools. In *ProQuest LLC eBooks*. https://eric.ed.gov/?id=ED555909

Aliprantis, D. (2023, June 1). *Public policy and the formation of residentially segregated cities.* Retrieved June 5, 2024, from https://www.clevelandfed.org/collections/conversations-on-economic-inclusion/2023/cei-20230505-state-of-racial-inequality-a-conversation-with-professor-richard-rothstein

Anguiano, D. (2021, October 22). California: 32,000 kids return to class on Monday after wildfires hit schools. *California | The Guardian*. Retrieved November 25, 2023, from https://amp.theguardian.com/us-news/2018/nov/30/california-wildfires-schools-paradise

APA Task Force on Urban Psychology. (2005). Report of the task force on urban psychology toward an urban psychology: Research, action, and policy. In *APA task force on urban psychology toward an urban psychology: Research, action, and policy* [Report]. Retrieved November 25, 2023, from https://www.apa.org/pi/ses/resources/publications/urban-taskforce.pdf

Berman, S. L., Kurtines, W. M., Silverman, W. K., & Serafini, L. T. (1996). The impact of exposure to crime and violence on urban youth. *American Journal of Orthopsychiatry*, *66*(3), 329–336. https://doi.org/10.1037/h0080183

Boell, M., & Senge, P. (2016, June 7). *School climate and social fields – An initial exploration – Garrison Institute*. Garrison Institute. Retrieved June 5, 2024, from https://www.garrisoninstitute.org/resource/school-climate-social-fields-initial-exploration/

Breslau, N., Chilcoat, H. D., Kessler, R. C., & Davis, G. C. (1999). Previous exposure to trauma and PTSD effects of subsequent trauma: Results from the Detroit Area Survey of Trauma. *The American Journal of Psychiatry*, *156*(6), 902–907. https://doi.org/10.1176/ajp.156.6.902

Brown, K. M., & Wynn, S. R. (2009). Finding, supporting, and keeping: The role of the principal in teacher retention issues. *Leadership and Policy in Schools*, *8*(1), 37–63. https://doi.org/10.1080/15700760701817371

Brumfield, B. (2012, December 18). Connecticut teachers were heroes in the face of death. *CNN*. Retrieved November 26, 2023, from https://www.cnn.com/2012/12/17/us/connecticut-shooting-teacher-heroism

Brunetti, G. J. (2006). Resilience under fire: Perspectives on the work of experienced, inner city high school teachers in the United States. *Teaching and Teacher Education*, *22*(7), 812–825. https://doi.org/10.1016/j.tate.2006.04.027

California, S. O. (n.d.). *SMARTER plan*. Coronavirus COVID-19 Response. Retrieved April 6, 2022, from https://covid19.ca.gov/smarter

Carver-Thomas, D., Kini, T., & Burns, D. (2020). *Sharpening the divide: How California's teacher shortages expand inequality*. Palo Alto, CA: Learning Policy Institute.

Children exposed to violence | National Institute of Justice. (2016, September 21). National Institute of Justice. https://nij.ojp.gov/topics/articles/children-exposed-violence

Cole, S. F., O'Brien, J.G., Gadd, M.G., Ristuccia, J., Wallace, D. L., & Gregory, M. (2005). *Helping traumatized children learn: Supportive school environments for children traumatized by family violence.* Boston: Massachusetts Advocates for Children.

Coles, D., Manassah, T., & Schwerner, C. (2022, April 7). Mental health crises are bombarding our schools. Here's what we can do (Opinion). *Education Week.* Retrieved November 25, 2023, from https://www.edweek.org/leadership/opinion-mental-health-crises-are-bombarding-our-schools-heres-what-we-can-do/2022/03

Darling-Hammond, L., & Darling-Hammond, S. (2024). Brown at 70: Progress, pushback, and policies that matter. Spencer Foundation, Learning Policy Institute, California Association of African-American Superintendents and Administrators.

EdTrust-West. (2015, October). *Black minds matter: Supporting the educational success of Black children in California – The Education Trust – West. The Education Trust – West.* Retrieved November 25, 2023, from https://west.edtrust.org/resource/black-minds-matter-supporting-the-educational-success-of-black-children-in-california/

Federal Housing Administration (FHA). (1938). Underwriting manual: Underwriting and valuation procedure under Title II of the National Housing Act | HUD USER. In *Hud user: Office of policy development and research (PD&R).* U.S. Government Printing Office. Retrieved April 21, 2024, from https://www.huduser.gov/portal/publications/Federal-Housing-Administration-Underwriting-Manual.html

Florida, R. L. (2017). *The new urban crisis: How our cities are increasing inequality, deepening segregation, and failing the middle class-and what we can do about it.* Retrieved June 5, 2024, from https://lib-jkt.sbm.itb.ac.id/index.php?p=show_detail&id=1746&keywords=

Frankenberg, E., Ee, J., Ayscue, J. B., & Orfield, G. (2019). Harming our common future: America's segregated schools 65 years after Brown. Retrieved June 5, 2024, from https://www.civilrightsproject.ucla.edu/research/k-12-education/integration-and-diversity/harming-our-common-future-americas-segregated-schools-65-years-after-brown

Fullan, M., & Quinn, J. (2015). *Coherence: the right drivers in action for schools, districts, and systems* (Kindle). Thousand Oaks, CA: Corwin Press.

George, J., & Darling-Hammond, L. (2019). *The federal role and school integration: Brown's promise and present challenges.* Palo Alto, CA: Learning Policy Institute.

Hart, S. L., Hodgkinson, S. C., Belcher, H. M. E., Hyman, C., & Cooley-Strickland, M. (2012). Somatic symptoms, peer and school stress, and family and community violence exposure among urban elementary school children. *Journal of Behavioral Medicine, 36*(5), 454–465. https://doi.org/10.1007/s10865-012-9440-2

Hill, A. C. (2011). *The cost of caring: An investigation in the effects of teaching traumatized children in urban elementary settings.* Amherst: University of Massachusetts Amherst.

Jiang, Y., Ekono, M., & Skinner, C. (2015). *Basic Facts about Low-Income Children: Children under 18 Years, 2013.* New York: National Center for Children in Poverty, Mailman School of Public Health, Columbia University.

Jones, C. (2021, August 13). How schools help students who've lost loved ones to Covid. *EdSource.* Retrieved March 19, 2024, from https://edsource.org/2021/how-schools-help-students-whove-lost-loved-ones-to-covid/659527?amp=1

Kirtman, L., & Fullan, M. (2016). *Key competencies for whole-system change.* Bloomington, IN: Solution Tree Press.

Learning Policy Institute (LPI). (2017). California teacher shortages: A persistent problem (fact sheet). Palo Alto, CA: Learning Policy Institute.

Mathews, K., Ph. D., & Hart Research Associates. (2022). Voices from the classroom: Developing a strategy for teacher retention and recruitment. Retrieved November 26, 2023, from https://transformschools.ucla.edu/wp-content/uploads/2022/10/Voices-from-the-Classroom-Developing-a-Strategy-for-Teacher-Retention-and-Recruitment.pdf

Meador, Derrick. (2018, June 14). How to become a school board member. *ThoughtCo.* Retrieved June 5, 2024, from https://www.thoughtco.com/how-to-become-school-board-member-3194408.

Michael Jr. (2017, January 9). *Know your why | Michael Jr.* [Video]. YouTube. Retrieved June 5, 2024, from https://www.youtube.com/watch?v=1ytFB8TrkTo

Mintzberg, H. (1979). *The structuring of organizations: A synthesis of the research.* Englewood Cliffs, NJ: Prentice-Hall.

National Center for Education Statistics (NCES). (2023). *Concentration of public-school students eligible for free or reduced-price lunch. Condition of education.* U.S. Department of Education, Institute of Education Sciences. Retrieved June 5, 2024, from https://nces.ed.gov/programs/coe/indicator/clb.

National Education Association (NEA). (2022). Solving educator shortages by making public education an attractive and competitive career path. In *Elevating the education professions.* Retrieved June 5, 2024, from https://www.nea.org/sites/default/files/2022-10/29302-solving-educator-shortage-report-final-oct-11-2022.pdf

National Housing Agency. (1946). U.S. National Housing Agency – A decade of housing. In *Hud User.* Retrieved April 21, 2024, from https://www.huduser.gov/portal/publications/Decade-of-Housing.html

National Public Radio, Inc. (NPR) (2017). *A 'forgotten history' of how the U.S. segregated America.* Retrieved April 21, 2024, from https://www.npr.org/templates/transcript/transcript.php?storyId=526655831

Nctsnadmin. (2018, May 30). *Addressing race and trauma in the classroom: A resource for educators.* The National Child Traumatic Stress Network. Retrieved April 21, 2024, from https://www.nctsn.org/resources/addressing-race-and-trauma-classroom-resource-educators

Ollison, J. (2019a, June). Improving teacher retention by addressing teachers' compassion fatigue. *Scholarly Commons.* Retrieved November 25, 2023, from https://scholarlycommons.pacific.edu/uop_etds/3602/

Ollison, J. (2019b, November 13). *Compassion fatigue | Jacquelyn Ollison | TEDxOhloneCollege* [Video]. YouTube – TEDx Talks. Retrieved November 25, 2023, from https://www.youtube.com/watch?v=-Cmc-5sU5L4

Orfield, G., & Pfleger, R. (2024, April 3). *The unfinished battle for integration in a multiracial America – From Brown to now – The Civil Rights Project at UCLA.* The Civil Rights Project. Retrieved April 21, 2024, from https://civilrightsproject.ucla.edu/research/k-12-education/integration-and-diversity/the-unfinished-battle-for-integration-in-a-multiracial-america-2013-from-brown-to-now

Osofsky, J. D., Hann, D. M., & Peebles, C. (1993). Adolescent parenthood: Risks and opportunities for mothers and infants. *APA PsycNet.* Retrieved November 25, 2023, from https://psycnet.apa.org/record/1993-98147-007

Podolsky, A., Kini, T., Bishop, J. B., & Darling-Hammond, L. (2016). *Solving the teacher shortage: How to attract and retain excellent educators.* Retrieved April 21, 2024, from https://doi.org/10.54300/262.960

Post-Traumatic Stress Disorder. (n.d.). Mental Health America. Retrieved November 5, 2023, from https://www.mhanational.org/conditions/post-traumatic-stress-disorder

Poverty – Healthy People 2030 | Health.gov. (n.d.). Retrieved November 5, 2023, from https://health.gov/healthypeople/priority-areas/social-determinants-health/literature-summaries/poverty

Reardon, S. F., & Bischoff, K. (2011). Income inequality and income segregation. *American Journal of Sociology, 116*(4), 1092–1153. https://doi.org/10.1086/657114

Reynolds, L. K., O'Koon, J. H., Papademetriou, E., Szczygiel, S., & Grant, K. E. (2001). Stress and somatic complaints in low-income urban adolescents. *Journal of Youth and Adolescence, 30*(4), 499–514. https://doi.org/10.1023/a:1010401417828

Rothstein, Richard. (2017). *The Color of Law: A Forgotten History of How Our Government Segregated America.* New York: Liveright Publishing Corporation. Kindle Edition.

Salancik, G. R., & Pfeffer, J. (1977). Who gets power — And how they hold on to it: A strategic-contingency model of power. *Organizational Dynamics, 5*(3), 3–21. https://doi.org/10.1016/0090-2616(77)90028-6

Schill, M. H., & Friedman, S. (1998). The Fair Housing Amendments Act of 1988: The first decade. *Cityscape: A Journal of Policy Development and Research, 4*, 57. Retrieved April 21, 2024, from https://www.huduser.gov/Periodicals/CITYSCPE/VOL4NUM3/schill.pdf

Schwartz, A. C., Bradley, R. L., Sexton, M., Sherry, A., & Ressler, K. J. (2005). Posttraumatic stress disorder among African Americans in an inner-city mental health clinic. *Psychiatric Services, 56*(2), 212–215. https://doi.org/10.1176/appi.ps.56.2.212

Stamm, B. H. (2010). *The concise ProQOL manual.* Pocatello, ID: ProQOL.org.

Sutcher, L., Carver-Thomas, D., & Darling-Hammond, L. (2018, February 5). *Understaffed and underprepared: California districts report ongoing teacher shortages.* Palo Alto, CA: Learning Policy Institute. https://learningpolicyinstitute.org/product/ca-district-teacher-shortage-brief

Thompson, T., & Massat, C. R. (2005). Experiences of violence, post-traumatic stress, academic achievement and behavior problems of urban African-American children. *Child & Adolescent Social Work Journal*, *22*(5–6), 367–393. https://doi.org/10.1007/s10560-005-0018-5

Walker, T. (2023, December 8). *'My empathy felt drained': Educators struggle with compassion fatigue | NEA*. Retrieved April 24, 2024, from https://www.nea.org/nea-today/all-news-articles/compassion-fatigue-teachers

2

Understanding Compassion Fatigue

In this chapter we will explore compassion fatigue as a combination of secondary trauma and burnout. This chapter will describe what it is and how it is measured, symptoms for individuals and organizations, factors that influence susceptibility and strategies to mitigate it. As you read, reflect on your personal and professional experiences with compassion fatigue.

What Is Compassion Fatigue?

Compassion fatigue is a perfect storm. It is the combination of secondary traumatic stress (STS) and burnout (Stamm, 2010; Treating Compassion Fatigue, 2002) (Figure 2.1). In this storm it is helpful to note that both can have negative consequences for the helping professional especially when you think of burnout as causing "feelings of hopelessness and difficulties in dealing with work or in doing your job effectively" (Stamm, 2010, p. 13) and STS in reference to "work-related, secondary exposure to people who have experienced extremely or traumatically stressful events" (p. 13).

FIGURE 2.1 Compassion Fatigue (Stamm, 2010)

Compassion fatigue refers to the detrimental effects one experiences on mental health because of helping others who suffer from trauma (Lerias & Byrne, 2003). That is, "the response of those persons who have witnessed, been subject to explicit knowledge of or, had the responsibility to intervene in a seriously distressing or tragic event" (Lerias & Byrne, 2003, p. 130).

Figley (1995) began writing about this phenomenon in the mid-1980s and spurred a movement to re-conceptualize trauma and those who suffer while supporting trauma victims coining the term compassion fatigue along the way. Research shows that helping professionals like therapists, social workers, first responders, and teachers are more vulnerable to compassion fatigue if they are working with victims of childhood trauma (Figley, 1995; Knight, 2013; Walker, 2023). The impact negatively affects their mental, psychological, emotional, and physical health (Knight, 2013). Terms such as "vicarious trauma," "secondary traumatic stress," "indirect trauma," and "compassion fatigue" are often used interchangeably to describe the impact to practitioners (Figley, 1995; Knight, 2013).

Compassion Fatigue Symptoms

As the symptoms are described please remember that these symptoms occur in response to witnessing the trauma of others because the whole premise of compassion fatigue is predicated on the secondhand transmission of traumatic experiences (Figley, 1995). You do not have to experience traumatic events firsthand to experience compassion fatigue. Additionally, symptoms will be shared in relation to STS and burnout.

A Brief Note on Secondary Traumatic Stress

While working with individuals who suffer from trauma, it is possible for the caregiver to absorb their client's trauma as if it is their own and suffer too (Figley 1995). It is argued that compassion fatigue is "identical to secondary traumatic stress disorder (STSD) and is the equivalent of PTSD" (Figley, 1995, p. xiv). Understanding compassion fatigue requires an understanding of trauma and in particular post-traumatic stress disorder (PTSD). The American Psychiatric Association's Diagnostic and Statistical Manual of Mental Disorders (4th Ed.) defines trauma as occurring when:

> The person has experienced an event outside the range of usual human experience that would be markedly distressing to almost anyone: a serious threat to his or her life or physical integrity; serious threat or harm to his children, spouse, or other close relatives or friends; sudden destruction of his home or community; or seeing another person seriously injured or killed in an accident or by physical violence.
>
> (As cited in Figley, 1995, p. xv)

PTSD is a psychological disorder that results from exposure to one or more traumatic events including witnessing trauma (APA, DSM-5 Task Force, 2013). These events include but are not limited to direct experience with or witnessing of war, physical assaults or attacks, robbery, childhood physical abuse, sexual abuse or violence, domestic violence, kidnapping, terrorism, torture, natural disasters, human disasters, medical catastrophes, suicide, serious injuries, and severe accidents (APA, DSM-5 Task Force, 2013).

Of note here is the reference to seeing another person's trauma (Figley, 1995; Lerias & Byrne, 2003). A person's perception of the experienced or witnessed trauma affects the severity of their PTSD response (Lerias & Byrne, 2003).

When one tries to help a trauma victim, be it from a client-patient relationship or some other significant relationship sometimes it can be stressful, so much so that the experience is called secondary traumatic stress (Figley, 1995). That is, "secondary trauma occurs when one is exposed to extreme events directly experienced by another" (Treating Compassion Fatigue, 2002, p. 124). STSD is "a syndrome of symptoms nearly identical to PTSD, except that exposure to knowledge about a traumatizing event experienced by a significant other is associated with the set of STSD symptoms, and PTSD symptoms are directly connected to the sufferer, the person experiencing primary traumatic stress" (Figley, 1995, p. 6). Put simply, compassion fatigue is the cost one pays when caring too much about a trauma victim. The cost is so impactful that one's mental health can suffer as a result. Individuals with PTSD may be quick tempered, aggressive, or reckless, engage in self-destructive behavior, or experience persistent dissociative symptoms of detachment from their bodies or the world around them and have trouble remembering daily events and attending to focused tasks (Diagnostic and statistical manual of mental disorders: DSM-5, 2013).

Symptoms of Compassion Fatigue Related to STS

The symptoms of compassion fatigue related to STS closely mirror PTSD symptoms (Bride et al., 2007; Figley, 1995). There are four main categories of symptoms for PTSD and secondary traumatic stress disorder (STSD). The categories are (a) reexperiencing the event, (b) persistent avoidance, (c) increased anxiety and arousal, and (d) negative changes in mood and thoughts which all lead to impairment (APA, DSM-5 Task Force, 2013; Bride et al., 2007; Fitzgerald, 2023; Lerias & Byrne, 2003; APA DSM-IV 4th Ed, as cited in Figley, 1995). Within each of the categories is a slew of harmful effects that can occur (Figley, 1995; Lerias & Byrne, 2003; Yassen, 1995). See Table 2.1.

Symptoms Associated with Persistent Avoidance
People with PTSD may go to great lengths to avoid situations, people, places, or conversations that remind them of the traumatic event (APA, DSM-5 Task Force, 2013). Persistent avoidance refers to deliberate but possibly unconscious attempts to avoid

TABLE 2.1 Reexperiencing Traumatic Event Symptoms

Symptoms associated with reexperiencing the traumatic event can include:

- Intrusive thoughts
- Disturbing or distressing daydreams and nightmares
- Flashbacks that involve feeling as though the traumatic event is happening again,
  - Often accompanied by a sense of reliving the experience
- Ill-timed recollections or reminders of the event
- Intense psychological distress or physiological reactivity in which individuals experience strong emotional reactions or physical sensations when exposed to reminders or triggers associated with the traumatic event

Source: APA, DSM-5 Task Force (2013); Lerias and Byrne (2003).

thinking, remembering details, concentrating, talking, or feelings about trauma (Lerias & Byrne, 2003). Social withdrawal from life events including from significant others is also avoidance behavior.

Symptoms Associated with Increased Anxiety and Arousal

Increased anxiety and arousal refer to hypervigilance or a heightened sense of awareness of one's environment to avoid danger and remain safe (Colman, 2006; Lerias & Byrne, 2003). Defining characteristics include attempts to stay awake or insomnia, anxiety, startled easily or jumpy, irritability and moodiness, prone to angry outbursts (Lerias & Byrne, 2003).

Symptoms Associated with Negative Mood Changes and Impairment

Negative alterations in mood and cognition can manifest as feelings of hopelessness regarding the future, memory issues that may involve the inability to recall crucial details of the traumatic event, challenges in sustaining meaningful relationships, and a sense of detachment from loved ones (Fitzgerald, 2023). Impairment is the total effect of the categories discussed above that impair one's ability to function normally at work, at home, and in social situations (Bride et al. 2007; Figley 1995; Lerias & Byrne, 2003; Wagaman et al., 2015; Yassen, 1995).

Additional Symptoms of Note
Can include the potential for the following:

- Self-harm.
- Withdrawal of intimacy.
- Hopelessness due to the lack of control of over the suffering of others.
- Intolerance.
- Physical illnesses such as sweating and rapid heartbeat.
- Confusion.
- Depression.
- And emotional numbness.

        (Wagaman et al. 2015; Yassen 1995)

Helping professionals who experience symptoms such as these are much less capable of serving those who are traumatized because of the trauma they are suffering themselves (Figley, 1995; Stamm, 1995; Wagaman et al., 2015). This means when you are suffering you aren't able to be the best teacher you want to be, and your students may suffer as a result.

 Pause and Reflect: *Are you experiencing any of the secondary traumatic stress symptoms described here? If so, what? Are they affecting your teaching in any way? If so, how?*

Burnout Symptoms

Research defines burnout as a "state of physical, emotional, and mental exhaustion caused by a depletion of ability to cope with one's environment resulting from our responses to the on-going demand characteristics (stress) of our daily lives (Maslach, 1982)" (Treating Compassion Fatigue, 2002, p. 125). It is a universal term that describes the chronic emotional response that can occur in humans, including helping professionals like teachers, who deal with others human beings who have extensive problems or troubles (Figley, 1995; Maslach, 2003; Newell & MacNeil, 2010).

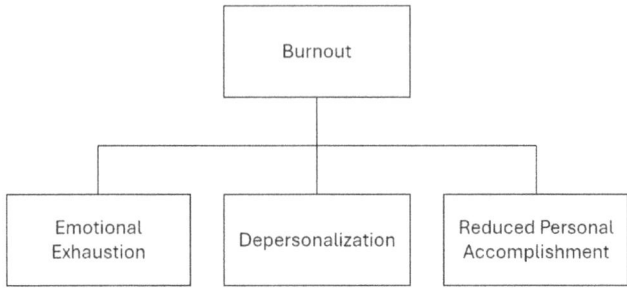

FIGURE 2.2 Burnout Symptoms (Maslach, 2003)

In Figure 2.2, one can see that burnout is also a syndrome comprised of three parts including "emotional exhaustion, depersonalization, and reduced personal accomplishment that can occur [over time] among individuals who do 'people-work' of some kind" (Maslach, 2003, p. 2). It is unique in that burnout is a response to the social interactions between people within work environments or other social situations (Figley, 1995; Maslach, 2003).

A Brief Note on Burnout

Take a moment to reflect on the word burnout. What comes to mind when you think of a burned-out teacher? When I picture a teacher who is burned out, I think of someone who is tired, overwhelmed, and generally unexcited to face a day of teaching children. It is not beautiful or loving or kind it just is. Burnout is complex (Maslach, 2003; Newell & MacNeil, 2010), and there exists a myriad of risk factors and symptoms that accompany burnout that teachers are privy to.

As the study of burnout has increased since its discovery in the mid-1970s by Christina Maslach and others the complexity of the syndrome has also grown. Research now shows, "Burnout arises from chronic mismatches between people and their work setting in terms of some or all of these six areas: workload, control, reward, community, fairness, and values" (Maslach et al., 2001, p. 441). The mismatch model shows burnout is likely if there exists an excessive workload, feelings of lack of control over resources or situations, few positive social connections, perceptions of unfairness, lack of mutual respect and trust, or a severe mismatch of values or beliefs that the work is unethical within the workplace in any combination thereof (Maslach et al., 2001). Moreover, these areas serve as a conceptual framework to help underscore the need to understand the cause of burnout as relative to the work context or setting (Maslach 2003; Maslach et al., 2001). *It is a job-related condition that can shift with a job change or changing nature of the work.*

These areas are also significant risk factors for the development of burnout in educators (Friedman, 1995). Burnout is also high among teachers in urban schools (Abel & Sewell, 1999; Farber, 1984). Mutual respect is vital in schools, but this may be disrupted when poor student behavior is of concern (Abel & Sewell, 1999; Brouwers & Tomic, 2000; Friedman, 1995). Though often said differently than Maslach et al. (2001), risk factors for teacher burnout are the same as those characterized in the mismatch model. That is teachers are at risk of burnout if they experience poor working conditions and/or poor staff relationship categories both of which encompass resources, workload, relationships, and respect to name a few (Abel & Sewell, 1999).

Emotional Exhaustion, Depersonalization, and Reduced Personal Accomplishment

Recall that burnout is characterized by both emotional exhaustion and depersonalization (CVT, n.d.; Newell & MacNeil, 2010; Maslach, 2003; Maslach & Jackson, 1981; Maslach et al., 2001).

Emotional exhaustion occurs when one allows themselves to become too emotionally invested in another human being to their detriment. This investment drains one of the energy reserves needed to deal with the emotions of others daily (Figley, 1995; Maslach, 2003). *Depersonalization* occurs when one begins to detach themselves from interacting too closely with others or those they serve. It is a defense mechanism employed to harden oneself in an attempt to put distance between oneself and other people – a protection mechanism (Figley et al., 1995; Maslach, 2003).

Unfortunately, depersonalization often results in diminished care and meaningful interaction with those whom the helping professional serves (Maslach, 2003; Maslach & Jackson, 1981).

The exhaustion and depersonalization result in "reduced personal accomplishment" (Maslach, 2003, p. 2) or self-efficacy which could manifest as a feeling of incompetence, inadequacy, and an inability to connect with others that allow for successful work – they feel like failures (Maslach, 2003; Maslach & Jackson, 1981). Put another way, reduced personal accomplishment is akin to one "feeling helpless or hopeless about your work and a sense of failure to reach your personal work-related goals" (Center for The Victims of Torture [CVT], n.d.).

Depersonalizing Protects Me

Randy, High School Teacher

In 2021, I almost died from COVID-19 and felt like my students could care less. One student even told me he thought I should have died. That was the last straw. These kids aren't worth it – well at least not him. So, I stopped caring or trying with him. He got zero effort from me. The sad thing is, while I lay in the hospital on my death bed, I thought about him and all my students – wondering how I could help them and get back to them. Mind you, it was a difficult class, and the students were dealing with a lot and their behavior certainly matched it but when he said I should have died – I just couldn't care anymore. I feel guilty about this because I know his life circumstances contribute to his behavior and affect. Dang, I can't let their heartbreaking lives affect my life anymore. Maybe someday this country will seriously address the deep systemic impact of generational poverty and harm, but I know it won't happen for a long – long time. So, I am going to keep it moving and do my best and not let their trauma become mine.

Other symptoms of burnout include cynicism, negativity, stress, anxiety, and blaming both of the self and those the helper is supposed to serve (Maslach, 2003). All these systems result in what Maslach (2003) calls a "pluralistic ignorance" (p. 17) meaning that people pretend they are doing fine and not experiencing burnout when they are. Pluralistic ignorance worsens helping professionals' feelings of isolation, leading them to feel as if they are the only person experiencing burnout so that they are unable to get the help they need (Maslach, 2003). The Center for The Victims of Torture [CVT], (n.d.) describes burnout similarly but offers more symptoms that are more practitioner focused. Table 2.2 includes the CVT's description of symptoms.

TABLE 2.2 Center for The Victims of Torture [CVT] Burnout Symptoms (n.d.)

Physical Symptoms
- Fatigue/exhaustion
- Headaches
- Sleep disturbances: difficulty falling or staying asleep increased/decreased sleep
- Digestive problems
- Increased physical complaints

Emotional & Cognitive Symptoms
- Emotional distress (e.g., feelings of sadness, depression)
- Anger and irritability
- Inwardly directed criticism
- Difficulty concentrating
- Increased cynicism or negativity
- Increased doubts and uncertainty

Behavioral Symptoms
- Excessive use of substances: nicotine, alcohol, illicit drugs
- Risk-taking

Work-Related Symptoms
- Avoidance or dread of working with certain patients or colleagues
- Withdrawing from colleagues
- Decreased job performance
- Negative attitude toward the job, organization, and/or patients
- Depersonalization
- Absenteeism
- Lack of satisfaction from achievements
- Decreased sense of personal accomplishment
- Feeling unable to help
- Disillusionment
- Reduced job commitment
- Reduced job motivation
- Low career satisfaction

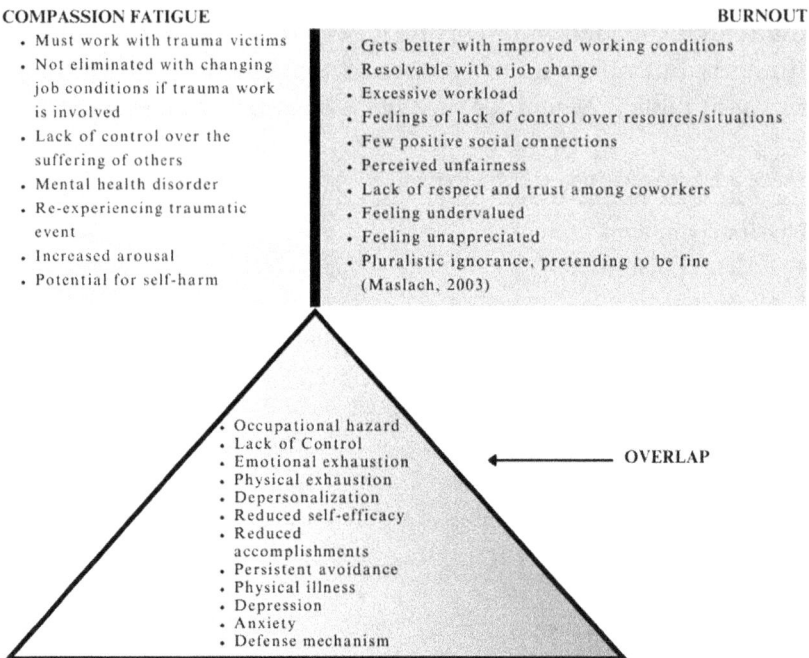

FIGURE 2.3 Parallels between Burnout and Compassion Fatigue

 Pause and Reflect: *Are you experiencing any of the burnout symptoms described here? If so, what? Are they affecting your teaching in any way? If so, how?*

The Parallels between Compassion Fatigue and Burnout

Understanding the difference between burnout and compassion fatigue can be perplexing given that they share many common overlapping characteristics. Research shows that burnout or the cumulative stress caregivers face negatively affects their resilience, making them more likely to experience compassion fatigue (Figley, 2002). Figure 2.3 illustrates the critical differences in the characteristics of compassion fatigue and burnout discussed in this chapter. The list of features is not exhaustive.

Compassion Fatigue Is an Occupational Hazard

Compassion fatigue is an occupational hazard (Adams et al., 2006; Figley, 1995; Jacobson, 2006; Newell & MacNeil, 2010). Burnout is also an occupational hazard (Maslach, 2003; Newell & MacNeil, 2010). Alone Burnout and STS are overwhelming personally and professionally, but combined as compassion fatigue they can be extremely difficult to handle especially if one is unaware, they are suffering from it. Understanding the nature of secondary trauma calls for training and awareness for all "helping professionals" who work with traumatized clients (Figley, 1995; Pearlman & Saakvitne, 1995).

> It is imperative that trauma workers' powers-that-be head the plea to acknowledge, the emotional consequences that may inhibit the vital work...preventative measures can be established to ensure that trauma workers will be able to meet their emotional needs (at work and home) to integrate job-induced STS.
> (Harris, 1995, p. 111)

Compassion Fatigue and Empathy

Helping professionals use empathy to connect with their client to better understand their issues (Figley, 1995; Valent, 1995; Wagaman et al., 2015). Doing this, however, puts the professional at risk of suffering from the same issues their clients are experiencing – the essence of compassion fatigue. Helping professionals who are unable to be empathic will likely not suffer from compassion fatigue, but they also will not be good at their jobs (Figley, 2002). "Empathy is the ability to understand what other people are feeling and thinking and is an essential skill in facilitating social agreement and successfully navigating personal relationships (de Waal, 2010; Toussaint & Webb, 2005)" (as cited in Wagaman et al., 2015, p. 203). It is a critical component of effective client-helping professional relationships (Wagaman et al., 2015). Helping professionals who consistently feel and express empathy to help others in distress will likely suffer from emotional and physical fatigue or compassion fatigue (Figley, 1995; Turgoose & Maddox, 2017).

For teachers, knowing and understanding the culture and backgrounds of students is key to effective teaching (Darling-Hammond, 2000; Delpit, 2006; Gay, 2002). That is, "the academic achievement of ethnically diverse students [urban] will improve when they are taught through their own cultural and experiential filters" (Gay, 2002, p. 106). In addition, empathy makes a teacher better too, but at a cost (Adams et al., 2006; Cooper, 2004; Figley, 2002). That is, teachers' effectiveness with students is increased when empathy is used, but overuse can have a detrimental effect on the teacher's belief in their ability to meet the academic and cultural needs of their students over time (Adams et al., 2006; Cooper, 2004).

Empathy Comes with the Job

Anna, Middle School Teacher

It is a struggle, setting boundaries, you know. How am I not supposed to feel for my students? I mean empathy comes with the job. The more I learn about the trauma my students experience the more I am affected. It stresses me out and I know it has led to my feelings of burnout. I wish I could turn it off and on, but I can't. Do you know any teachers who can? When my students choose to tell me about their lives, I am not going to NOT listen to them. And because of that I am affected. The students can't help their lives and because of the nature of my job I can't help mine. No one said teaching was easy. But it would be nice if other people besides teachers knew that.

 Pause and Reflect: *Are you an empathetic teacher?*

Characteristics of Helping Professionals Prone to Compassion Fatigue

In a literature review of 32 studies to determine the factors associated with compassion fatigue in mental health professionals, Turgoose and Maddox (2017) found ten factors that influence susceptibility to compassion fatigue, though some more than others. The main factors included the professionals' own trauma history, mindfulness, empathy, and caseload, as well as other Professional

Compassion Fatigue Susceptibility Factors

- Professionals' Own Trauma History
  - *(Personally Experienced or Unresolved, First-hand Trauma)*
- Lack Of Mindfulness or Spiritual Practice
- Empathy Fatigue
- Large Caseload
  - *(Large Numbers of Traumatized Clients)*
- Burnout
- Compassion Satisfaction
  - *(Liking and Feeling Effective at Job)*
- Gender
  - *(Females More Susceptible Than Males)*

FIGURE 2.4 Compassion Fatigue Susceptibility Factors

Quality of Life Scale (ProQOL) variables: burnout and compassion satisfaction. Other variables that were investigated report very mixed results and as such do not appear to consistently influence compassion fatigue, such as age, sex[gender], religion, and work experience (p. 180). See Figure 2.4.

A few of the characteristics require further explanation. If someone has experienced trauma or has unresolved trauma, they are susceptible to compassion fatigue (Figley, 1995; Turgoose & Maddox, 2017). Mindfulness as a protective factor can stave off compassion fatigue, but in its absence, the opposite is true (Turgoose & Maddox, 2017). Helping professionals with large caseloads of traumatized patients were likely to suffer from compassion fatigue, too (Turgoose & Maddox, 2017).

Experience and age showed mixed results in that the longer a mental health professional worked with child victims of trauma, the more likely they were to suffer from compassion fatigue, which also means that the worker tended to be older. Results were mixed though in that more experience also led to decreased levels of compassion fatigue. Turgoose and Maddox (2017) hypothesized that more experienced professionals were given harder caseloads which could account for the variance. Unfortunately, the opposite is often true in education as the teacher shortage means that less experienced teachers are working with students who need more support (Carver-Thomas & Darling-Hammond, 2017). Lastly, religion and gender also showed mixed results (Turgoose & Maddox, 2017).

The ability to predict compassion fatigue varied greatly with some studies saying females are more susceptible than males and vice versa. Of note was that no religion tended to result in higher rates of compassion fatigue, though two studies found the opposite especially when used as a coping strategy (Turgoose and Maddox, 2017). While Turgoose and Maddox's (2017) review focused on mental health care professionals, the results are consistent with other studies of compassion fatigue in helping professions (Figley, 1995, 2002). What makes a person no longer able to bear the suffering of others or to be compassionate is key in understanding the features that can predict the onset of compassion fatigue (Figley, 2002; Turgoose & Maddox, 2017), in helping not only professionals but the teaching profession as well.

 Pause and Reflect: *Do you recognize any of these characteristics in yourself? If so, which ones?*

An Eye Toward Prevention

The best prevention for both compassion fatigue and burnout is early prevention in the form of awareness (National Child Traumatic Stress Network Schools Committee, 2008). Early awareness can occur by incorporating information about burnout and compassion fatigue into helping profession training programs like what has occurred for social workers and therapists (Adams et al., 2006; Figley, 1995; Jacobson, 2006; Maslach, 2003; Newell & MacNeil, 2010;). Practices such as support groups, professional development, stress management, and relaxation techniques also help to reduce the effects of compassion fatigue and burnout (Figley, 1995, 2002; Maslach, 2003; Newell & MacNeil, 2010; Stamm, 2010). With regard to schools, these practices would have to be implemented systemically within the structure of the school system and most likely from the strategic apex or superintendent level as they would require an infusion of new policy direction within the system (Mintzberg, 1979). But you don't have to wait for them to get started on your prevention journey.

Tool 2.1 – Awareness Is Half the Battle

Description: A tool to help you understand whether compassion fatigue might affect your professional quality of life.

Overview: Part of understanding our own compassion fatigue healing journey as a teacher is becoming aware of whether you are experiencing it. A free tool that can help you do that is the Professional Quality of Life Scale (5) (ProQOL 5.0) available at https://proqol.org/proqol-measure.

What: The ProQOL 5.0, as described by Stamm (2010), is a prominent measure for assessing the positive and negative effects of working with those who have faced highly stressful events. While ProQOL 5.0 is not diagnostic, elevated scores on burnout and STS can signal potential issues. Originally known as the Compassion Fatigue Self-Test from the late 1980s by Charles Figley, it encompasses two facets: compassion satisfaction (positive) and compassion fatigue (negative). The latter divides into burnout and secondary traumatic stress (STS) components. It is a free resource created by Stamm (2010) that is now owned by **The Center for Victims of Torture (CVT).** Visit www.ProQOL.org to learn more.

Directions:

1. Spend a few moments, about two to five minutes, engaging in deep breathing.
2. Navigate to the https://proqol.org/proqol-measure website and complete the ProQOL 5.0 assessment.
3. Reflect on your results by completing the following journal prompt: Were the results what you expected them to be? Why or why not?
4. Talk about the results with some you care about. Seek professional support if need be.

Please note: CVT specifies the ProQOL 5.0's usage conditions, including due credit, no alterations except for target group relevance, and no sales unless permission is sought. Permission was sought and granted. So, for this reason, the target group was shifted to teachers.

Professional Quality of Life Scale (ProQOL)

Compassion Satisfaction and Compassion Fatigue (ProQOL) Version 5 (2009)

Visit www.ProQOL.org to learn more about this assessment.

When you *[teach]* people you have direct contact with their lives. As you may have found, your compassion for those you *[teach]* can affect you in positive and negative ways. Below are some questions about your experiences, both positive and negative, as a *[teacher]*. Consider each of the following questions about you and your current work situation. Select the number that honestly reflects how frequently you experienced these things in the *last 30 days*.

1 = Never   2 = Rarely   3 = Sometimes   4 = Often   5 = Very Often

_____ 1. I am happy.
_____ 2. I am preoccupied with more than one person I *[teach]*.
_____ 3. I get satisfaction from being able to *[teach]* people.
_____ 4. I feel connected to others.
_____ 5. I jump or am startled by unexpected sounds.
_____ 6. I feel invigorated after working with those I *[teach]*.
_____ 7. I find it difficult to separate my personal life from my life as a *[teacher]*.
_____ 8. I am not as productive at work because I am losing sleep over traumatic experiences of a person I [teach].
_____ 9. I think that I might have been affected by the traumatic stress of those I *[teach]*.
_____ 10. I feel trapped by my job as a *[teacher]*.
_____ 11. Because of my *[teaching]*, I have felt "on edge" about various things.
_____ 12. I like my work as a *[teacher]*.
_____ 13. I feel depressed because of the traumatic experiences of the people I *[teach]*.
_____ 14. I feel as though I am experiencing the trauma of someone I have *[taught]*.
_____ 15. I have beliefs that sustain me.
_____ 16. I am pleased with how I am able to keep up with *[teaching]* techniques and protocols.
_____ 17. I am the person I always wanted to be.
_____ 18. My work makes me feel satisfied.
_____ 19. I feel worn out because of my work as a *[teacher]*.

_____ 20.   I have happy thoughts and feelings about those I *[teach]* and how I could teach them.
_____ 21.   I feel overwhelmed because my case [work] load seems endless.
_____ 22.   I believe I can make a difference through my work.
_____ 23.   I avoid certain activities or situations because they remind me of frightening experiences of the people I *[teach]*.
_____ 24.   I am proud of what I can do to *[teach]*.
_____ 25.   As a result of my *[teaching]*, I have intrusive, frightening thoughts.
_____ 26.   I feel "bogged down" by the system.
_____ 27.   I have thoughts that I am a "success" as a *[teacher]*.
_____ 28.   I can't recall important parts of my work with trauma victims.
_____ 29.   I am a very caring person.
_____ 30.   I am happy that I chose to do this work.

 Pause and Reflect: *Of the prevention recommendations listed here: support groups, professional development, stress management, and relaxation techniques, which one feels like something you might like to try? Why?*

Supports and Interventions That Help Combat Burnout

Although people may want to isolate themselves if they are experiencing burnout, more social interaction is called for especially with peers to improve burnout (Maslach, 2003). Peers provide insights, validation, barometers of delusion, humor, emotional support, and companionship that one cannot get alone (Maslach, 2003). In addition, finding the right job match helps. A good match includes a "sustainable workload, feelings of choice and control, appropriate recognition and reward, a supportive work community, fairness and justice, and meaningful and valued work" (Maslach et al., 2001, p. 417). Maslach et al. (2001) also advocate for focusing on the mismatches of value and reward as one way to combat burnout given that these areas make the other mismatches more palatable. Educators in urban schools are often mismatched with the work setting. For example, teachers with the least amount of experience and preparation to work in urban schools are tapped to teach students who need the most support (Podolsky & Sutcher, 2016).

Urban teachers are also most likely to be female, and of a different ethnicity than those they teach, which can hinder the sense of connection and relationship felt with students (Haberman, 2005). Moreover, the lack of staff diversity can diminish the potential for powerful collegial connections, which is another factor in urban teacher burnout (Barmore, 2021; Simon et al., 2015). Research shows that race matters when it comes to job satisfaction (Fairchild et al., 2012). When a teacher's students are not from the same ethnic group as the teacher, the teacher is often less satisfied with their job (Fairchild et al., 2012). This notion is concerning given that the majority of teachers are White and urban school students are majority non-White.

Lastly, as burnout is one part of the equation representing compassion fatigue, it is important to note that burnout is situational (Adams et al., 2006; Bride et al., 2007; Figley, 1995; Maslach, 2003). If job conditions are improved then burnout is reduced and can likely be eliminated (Maslach 2003; Maslach et al., 2001). That is, "such a focus allows for the possibility that the nature of the job may precipitate burnout and not just the nature of the person performing that job" (Maslach, 2003, p. 14). This last sentiment expressed by Maslach (2003) underscores hope for the working professional suffering from burnout in that burnout is not his or her fault, it is the working conditions that cause the suffering. So, let's change the working conditions.

Compassion Satisfaction – Teaching Is Not All Bad

It is important to note that helping those who are traumatized is also incredibly rewarding and satisfying (Stamm, 2010). This reward is known as compassion satisfaction or "the fulfillment from helping others and positive collegial relationships" (Conrad & Kellar-Guenther, 2006, p. 1072). Suffice to say, those who care for others as a career do so because they want to and compassion fatigue and compassion satisfaction are inversely correlated (Alkema et al., 2008; Conrad & Kellar-Guenther, 2006; Stamm,

2010). That is, when one receives positive reinforcement from their work, they are more likely "to experience happy thoughts, feel successful, are happy with the work they do, want to continue to do it, and believe they can make a difference," thus experiencing satisfaction (Stamm, 2010, p. 21). The possibility of compassion fatigue exists in the absence of this positivity (Stamm, 2010). School system leaders and those that influence the system externally and internally can play a significant role in ensuring that the conditions that create compassion fatigue shift, so that compassion satisfaction is more of the norm within urban schools (insert Cottrell, 2016; Fullan & Quinn, 2016; Mintzberg, 1979; Salancik & Pfeffer, 1977).

Shift the Conditions via School Climate

A school's working conditions and climate are also associated with teachers' attitudes, beliefs, or feelings toward their job (insert Berry et al. 2019; Collie et al., 2012). For example, Quartz et al. (2003) assert that 64% of teachers working in high-poverty urban schools do so because they want to help kids in urban communities. This type of desire or attitudinal belief is research supported. There exists a relationship between teacher job satisfaction and work-related attitudes (Fairchild et al., 2012). Positive feelings toward supervisor support, procedural justice, autonomy, job stress, and teacher-student relationships are linked with teacher job satisfaction (Fairchild et al., 2012; p. 174).

Understanding school climate in terms of feelings is also research supported. For example, Freiburg (1999) describes school climate as a quality that "helps each individual feel personal worth, dignity, and importance, while simultaneously helping create a sense of belonging to something beyond ourselves." He further reasons that "the climate of a school can foster resilience or become a risk factor in the lives of people who work and learn in a place called school" (p. 12). School climate is often described as the character and quality of a school (Collie et al., 2012; National School Climate Council, 2007). Given that compassion fatigue, sufferers often try to avoid feelings, it is plausible that teachers with compassion fatigue would be unable to feel anything about their school's climate and working conditions (Lerias & Byrne,

2003). Indeed, if they did it would be through a lens of empathic exhaustion and therefore unlikely to be positive (Turgoose & Maddox, 2017; Figley, 1995). Working in ways to improve working conditions and school climate has a positive impact on teachers and students in the school alike (Berry et al. 2019).

 Connect the Thoughts

1. What feelings or insights did you have to the information presented in this chapter?
2. How would you personally define compassion fatigue?
3. What surprising or significant knowledge did you gain from this chapter?
4. How do the ideas and information shared here connect to your existing knowledge or personal experiences with secondary trauma or burnout?
5. What new ideas broadened your perspective or introduced new challenges or puzzles for you?

References

Abel, M. H., & Sewell, J. (1999). Stress and burnout in rural and urban secondary school teachers. *The Journal of Educational Research/Journal of Educational Research*, *92*(5), 287–293. Retrieved November 26, 2023, from https://doi.org/10.1080/00220679909597608

Adams, R. E., Boscarino, J. A., & Figley, C. R. (2006). Compassion fatigue and psychological distress among social workers: A validation study. *American Journal of Orthopsychiatry*, *76*(1), 103.

Alkema, K., Linton, J. M., & Davies, R. (2008). A study of the relationship between self-care, compassion satisfaction, compassion fatigue, and burnout among hospice professionals. *Journal of Social Work in End-of-Life & Palliative Care*, *4*(2), 101–119.

American Psychiatric Association (APA), DSM-5 Task Force. (2013). *Diagnostic and statistical manual of mental disorders: DSM-5TM* (5th ed.). American Psychiatric Publishing, Inc. Retrieved November 26, 2023, from https://psycnet.apa.org/doi/10.1176/appi.books.9780890425596

Barmore, P. (2021, May 24). Black teachers are facing racial battle fatigue on top of a stressful job. *The Hechinger Report*. Retrieved June 4, 2024, from https://hechingerreport.org/black-teachers-ground-down-by-racial-battle-fatigue-after-a-year-like-no-other/

Berry, B., Bastian, K. C., Darling-Hammond, L., & Kini, T. (2019). *How teaching and learning conditions affect teacher retention and school performance in North Carolina*. Palo Alto, CA: Learning Policy Institute.

Bride, B. E., Radey, M., & Figley, C. R. (2007). Measuring compassion fatigue. *Clinical Social Work Journal*, *35*(3), 155–163.

Brouwers, A., & Tomic, W. (2000). A longitudinal study of teacher burnout and perceived self-efficacy in classroom management. *Teaching and Teacher Education*, *16*(2), 239–253. https://doi.org/10.1016/s0742-051x(99)00057-8

Carver-Thomas, D. & Darling-Hammond, L. (2017). *Teacher turnover: Why it matters and what we can do about it*. Palo Alto, CA: Learning Policy Institute. https://doi.org/10.54300/454.278.

Center for The Victims of Torture [CVT]. (n.d.). *Burnout*. Retrieved June 9, 2024, from https://proqol.org/burnout

Collie, R. J., Shapka, J. D., & Perry, N. E. (2012). School climate and social-emotional learning: Predicting teacher stress, job satisfaction, and teaching efficacy. *Journal of Educational Psychology*, *104*(4), 1189–1204. Retrieved June 4, 2024, from https://doi.org/10.1037/a0029356

Colman, A. M. (2006). *Oxford dictionary of psychology*. New York: Oxford University Press. Retrieved June 30, 2017, from Good Therapy Website, https://www.goodtherapy.org/blog/psychpedia/hypervigilance.

Conrad, D., & Kellar-Guenther, Y. (2006). Compassion fatigue, burnout, and compassion satisfaction among Colorado child protection workers. *Child Abuse & Neglect*, *30*(10), 1071–1080.

Cooper, B. (2004). Empathy, interaction, and caring: Teachers' roles in a constrained environment. *Pastoral Care in Education*, *22*(3), 12–21.

Cottrell, L. (2016). Joy and happiness: A simultaneous and evolutionary concept analysis. *Journal of Advanced Nursing, 72*(7), 1506–1517. Retrieved June 4, 2024 from https://doi.org/10.1111/jan.12980

Darling-Hammond, L. (2000). How teacher education matters. *Journal of Teacher Education*, *51*(3), 166–173.

Delpit, L. (2006). *Other people's children: Cultural conflict in the classroom*. The New Press.

Diagnostic and statistical manual of mental disorders: DSM-5 (5th ed.). (2013). Arlington, VA: American Psychiatric Association.

Farber, B. A. (1984). Teacher burnout: Assumptions, myths, and issues. *Teachers College Record*, *86*(2), 321–338. Retrieved June 4, 2024, from https://doi.org/10.1177/016146818408600207

Fairchild, S., Tobias, R., Corcoran, S., Djukic, M., Kovner, C., & Noguera, P. (2012). White and Black teachers' job satisfaction: Does relational demography matter? *Urban Education*, *47*(1), 170–197. Retrieved June 4, 2024, from https://doi.org/10.1177/0042085911429582

Figley, C. R. (1995). Compassion fatigue as secondary traumatic stress disorder: An overview. In C. R. Figley (Ed.) *Compassion fatigue: Coping with secondary traumatic stress disorder in those who treat the traumatized* (Psychosocial Stress Series) (Vol. 1, pp. 1–18) (Kindle Edition). New York: Taylor and Francis.

Figley, C. R. (ed.) (2002). *Treating compassion fatigue*. New York: Brunner-Routledge. https://doi.org/10.4324/9780203890318

Fitzgerald, A. (2023). *Somatic therapy for post-traumatic stress disorder. Understanding the body's role in healing trauma: Bridging mind and body with innovative therapies for trauma survivors* (Kindle Edition). UNITEXTO Digital Publishing.

Freiberg, H. J. (1999). *School climate: Measuring, improving and sustaining healthy learning environments* (1st ed.). New York: Routledge. https://doi.org/10.4324/9780203983980

Friedman, I. A. (1995). Student behavior patterns contributing to teacher burnout. *The Journal of Educational Research*, *88*(5), 281–289. Retrieved June 4, 2024, from https://doi.org/10.1080/00220671.1995.9941312

Fullan, M., & Quinn, J. (2015). *Coherence: The right drivers in action for schools, districts, and systems* (Kindle). Thousand Oaks, CA: Corwin Press.

Gay, G. (2002). Preparing for culturally responsive teaching. *Journal of Teacher Education*, *53*(2), 106–116. Retrieved June 4, 2024, from https://doi.org/10.1177/0022487102053002003

Haberman, M. (2005). Teacher burnout in black and white. *The New Educator*, *1*(3), 153–175. Retrieved June 4, 2024, from https://doi.org/10.1080/15476880590966303

Harris, N. B. (2021). *California surgeon general's playbook: Stress relief during COVID-19*. California Office of the California Surgeon General.

Retrieved June 4, 2024, from https://osg.ca.gov/wp-content/uploads/sites/266/2022/05/california-surgeon-general_stress-busting-playbook.pdf

Jacobson, J. M. (2006). Compassion fatigue, compassion satisfaction, and burnout: Reactions among employee assistance professionals providing workplace crisis intervention and disaster management services. *Journal of Workplace Behavioral Health*, *21*(3–4), 133–152.

Knight, C. (2013). Indirect trauma: Implications for self-care, supervision, the organization, and the academic institution. *The Clinical Supervisor*, *32*(2), 224–243. Retrieved June 4, 2024, from https://doi.org/10.1080/07325223.2013.850139

Lerias, D., & Byrne, M. K. (2003). Vicarious traumatization: Symptoms and predictors. *Stress and Health*, *19*(3), 129–138. Retrieved November 26, 2023, from https://doi.org/10.1002/smi.969

Maslach, C. (2003). *Burnout: Tthe cost of caring* (Kindle). MALOR ISHK. Retrieved November 26, 2023, from https://ci.nii.ac.jp/ncid/BA85645777 (Original work published 1982).

Maslach, C., & Jackson, S. E. (1981). The measurement of experienced burnout. *Journal of Organizational Behavior*, *2*(2), 99–113.

Maslach, C., Schaufeli, W. B., & Leiter, M. P. (2001). Job burnout. *Annual Review of Psychology*, *52*(1), 397–422.

Mintzberg, H. (1979). *The structuring of organizations: A synthesis of the research*. Englewood Cliffs, NJ: Prentice-Hall. Print.

National Child Traumatic Stress Network Schools Committee. (2008). *Child trauma toolkit for educators*. National Center for Child Traumatic Stress. Retrieved June 24, 2024, from https://www.nctsn.org/sites/default/files/resources//child_trauma_toolkit_educators.pdf

National School Climate Council. (2007). *The school climate challenge: Narrowing the gap between school climate research and school climate policy, practice guidelines and teacher education policy*. Retrieved from June 24, 2024, https://www.schoolclimate.org/climate/documents/policy/school-climate-challenge-web.pdf

Newell, J. M., & MacNeil, G. A. (2010). Professional burnout, vicarious trauma, secondary traumatic stress, and compassion fatigue: A review of theoretical terms, risk factors, and preventive methods for clinicians and researchers. *Best Practices in Mental Health*, *6*(2), 57–68.

Pearlman, L. A., & Saakvitne, K. W. (1995). *Treating therapists with vicarious traumatization and secondary traumatic stress disorders*. Retrieved November 26, 2023, from https://psycnet.apa.org/record/1995-97891-008

Podolsky, A., & Sutcher, L. (2016, November 30). *California Teacher shortages: a persistent problem*. Learning Policy Institute. Retrieved June 24, 2024, from https://learningpolicyinstitute.org/product/ca-teacher-shortage-persistent-problem-brief

Quartz, K. H., Olsen, B., & Duncan-Andrade, J. (2003). The *fragility of urban teaching: A longitudinal study of career development and activism*. UCLA's Institute for Democracy, Education, & Access.

Salancik, G. R., & Pfeffer, J. (1977). Who gets power—And how they hold on to it: A strategic-contingency model of power. *Organizational Dynamics*, *5*(3), 3–21. Reprinted from Organizational Dynamics, Winter 1977.

Simon, N. S., Johnson, S. M., & Reinhorn, S. K., & The Project on the Next Generation of Teachers. (2015). The challenge of recruiting and hiring teachers of color: Lessons from six High-Performing, High-Poverty, Urban Schools. In *Working Paper*. Harvard Graduate School of Education. Retrieved June 24, 2024, from https://projectngt.gse.harvard.edu/files/gse-projectngt/files/the_challenge_of_recruiting_and_hiring_teachers_of_color_diversity_july_2015.pdf

Stamm, B. (Ed.) (1995). *Secondary traumatic stress: Self-care issues for clinicians, researchers, and educators* (2nd ed.). Lutherville, MD: The Sidran Press.

Stamm, B. H. (2010). *The concise ProQOL manual* (2nd ed.). Pocatello, ID: ProQOL.org.

Turgoose, D., & Maddox, L. (2017). Predictors of compassion fatigue in mental health professionals: A narrative review. *Traumatology*, *23*(2), 172–185. https://doi.org/10.1037/trm0000116

Valent, P. (1995). Survival strategies: A framework for understanding secondary traumatic stress and coping in helpers. *Compassion fatigue: Coping with secondary traumatic stress disorder in those who treat the traumatized* (pp. 21–50) New York: Routledge.

Wagaman, M. A., Geiger, J. M., Shockley, C., & Segal, E. A. (2015). The role of empathy in burnout, compassion satisfaction, and secondary traumatic stress among social workers. *Social Work*, *60*(3), 201–209.

Walker, T. (2023, December 8). *'My empathy felt drained': Educators struggle with compassion fatigue | NEA*. Retrieved April 24, 2024, from https://www.nea.org/nea-today/all-news-articles/compassion-fatigue-teachers

Yassen, J. (1995). Preventing secondary. In *Compassion fatigue: Coping with secondary traumatic stress disorder in those who treat the traumatized* (Vol. 23, p. 178). New York: Routledge.

3

Research Shows Teachers Suffer from Compassion Fatigue

In this chapter we will explore research I conducted on teachers' experience with compassion fatigue from two studies. The goal of each study was to shed light on the types of experiences teachers are having with compassion fatigue to find solutions that can be instituted to help teachers to combat compassion fatigue and improve teacher retention. As you read, again reflect on your personal and professional experiences with compassion fatigue. Do you see yourself reflected in this research?

Why Study Teachers Experience Compassion Fatigue?

The substantial number of teachers leaving the Prek-12 teaching profession is concerning to say the least. Research shows that between 19% and 30% of new teachers leave teaching within the first five years and that rate can be as high as about 55% in high-poverty schools (Johnson, 2023; Podolsky et al., 2016). In other words, about **one out of every four** teachers leave the profession within five years and **one out of every two** leave if they are working at a high-poverty school. This is cringeworthy especially when you think about all the students who are impacted by the revolving door of teachers. Even more so when you understand that high-poverty students who are typically African American and Hispanic students in the United States are bearing the brunt of this high turnover (Cid-Martinez et al., 2023; Moore, 2022). On paper it does not sound as devastating but when we recognize that there are real people attached to these numbers it is heartbreaking. What is more, according to Mathews and Hart Research Associates (2022):

> Teacher retention will be a challenge in the near term. Four in ten current teachers have explored leaving the classroom either to continue within education or to switch occupations entirely. One in five current teachers say they will likely leave the profession in the next three years. Current teachers aged 55 and older are the most inclined to leave teaching within three years but more than one-third of younger teachers have a similar outlook.
> (p. 3)

I was a principal at a high-poverty school, and I saw firsthand the toll that not having a qualified teacher had on students. One year, I was having a tough time finding a permanent math teacher and had to fill the position with substitute teachers until I found one. That year, those students had four substitute teachers over the course of the entire year. Just imagine, that is one full year of academic learning that these students will never get back. It made me feel sad, angry, and powerless because there was not much that could be done about it until I was able to find a qualified teacher willing to take the position. I know that I am not alone in feeling this way. There are too many initiatives aimed at addressing the shortage of teachers by recruiting more teachers into the profession to address the constant turnover for that to be true.

There is no need to wonder why people are leaving because extensive research shows the most often cited reasons people leave the profession include difficult working conditions, low pay, and burnout (Mathews & Hart Research Associates, 2022; Podolsky et al., 2016). Mathews and Hart Research Associates (2022) further showed that "workload, low pay, student apathy and behavioral issues, and the lack of support from district administrators" contributes to teacher stress (p. 3). And yet, compassion fatigue is still not mentioned. And I think that is in large part because it is not as widely recognized as a reason teachers leave the teaching profession as it should be.

Research shows that stress levels and burnout can impact a teacher's perception of school climate, and since compassion fatigue is a stress response to trauma (Stamm, 2010), it is plausible that compassion fatigue can impact a teacher's ability to see their school's climate and working conditions positively (Rubinstein & McCarthy, 2016). To explore if this sentiment was true, I conducted two studies on compassion fatigue in educators. The goal of each study was to influence education policy agendas addressing the teacher shortage by shedding light on the types of support services school districts and policymakers can institute to combat compassion fatigue and improve urban educator retention with solutions based on school conditions and climate improvements. The inquiry provided data that could be acted on promptly in all schools throughout the United States should one choose to do so.

Key Questions

The first study conducted in 2018 included three key questions:

1. To what extent do California urban schoolteachers experience compassion fatigue?
2. How does compassion fatigue impact teachers' perception of their schools' working conditions and climate?
3. What organizational support can be put in place to help urban educators suffering from compassion fatigue thrive?

The second study, conducted in 2022, included teachers and administrators, was designed to explore the potential impact of the COVID-19 pandemic on the experience of compassion fatigue among California school teachers and administrators. Key questions for the that study were as follows:

1. In what ways does pandemic-influenced compassion fatigue affect educators' ability to create school climates beneficial to successful teaching and learning?

2. What coping behaviors are educators utilizing to combat the effects of pandemic-influenced compassion fatigue?
3. How does pandemic-influenced compassion fatigue impact educators' perception of their school's climate and working conditions?
4. What system supports, practices, and policies can be put in place to support educators who are experiencing pandemic-influenced compassion fatigue?

What follows is a synopsis of the quantitative and qualitative results of each study and a few illustrative vignettes derived from the research.

Synopsis of First Study: 2018–2019

Methodology
I conducted a mixed-methods action research study. The study had three cycles of action – Cycle 1 involved giving a survey to teachers, Cycle 2 consisted of follow-up interviews with teacher, and Cycle 3 was a series of facilitated discussions with education leaders – so that I could develop a comprehensive set of recommendations for combatting compassion fatigue. Each cycle was based on an emerging design that shifted at times during the process of engaging in the research. The emerging nature of the design was inherent given the fluid nature of action research (Herr & Anderson, 2015). Each cycle was planned to meet the quality and validity criteria of action research as articulated by Herr and Anderson (2015).

Measure
The "Professional Quality of Life: Compassion Satisfaction and Fatigue Version 5 (ProQOL 5) Scale" was administered to teachers throughout the state of California, and subsequent follow-up interviews were conducted. The ProQOL 5, as described by Stamm (2010), is a prominent measure for assessing the positive and negative effects of working with those who have faced highly stressful events. While the ProQOL 5 isn't diagnostic, elevated scores on burnout and STS can signal potential issues. Originally known as the Compassion Fatigue Self-Test from the

late 1980s by Charles Figley (1995), it encompasses two facets: compassion satisfaction (CS)(positive) and compassion fatigue (negative). The latter divides into burnout (BO) and secondary traumatic stress (STS) components.

Stamm specifies the ProQOL 5's usage conditions, including due credit, no alterations except for target group relevance, and no sales. Accordingly, for this study, the target group was shifted to teachers. The ProQOL 5 contains 30 Likert scale items, with results segmented into compassion satisfaction, secondary trauma, and burnout. The scoring process is a three-tiered approach:

1. Compassion Satisfaction: Sum of items 3, 6, 12, 16, 18, 20, 22, 24, 27, and 30.
2. Burnout: Reverse score items 1, 4, 15, 17, and 29, then sum with items 8, 10, 19, 21, and 26.
3. Secondary traumatic stress (STS): Sum of items 2, 5, 7, 9, 11, 13, 14, 23, 25, and 28.

The ProQOL 5 boasts sound construct validity, with interscale correlations demonstrating distinct variance between burnout and STS. Additionally, a demographic questionnaire accompanies the ProQOL 5, as per Stamm's recommendations, to enhance the study's depth.

Data Analysis

A descriptive statistical analysis was conducted to determine the characteristics of the educator sample in this study. Analysis of variance (ANOVA), Pearson's r correlation statistics, and linear and multiple regression were utilized to analyze the data (Ollison, 2019a; Johnson & Christensen, 2016). Ollison (2019a) showed that ANOVA can be used to identify statistically significant variances within teacher groups in compassion satisfaction and fatigue scores based on factors such as school site level, gender, ethnicity, and years in the profession. I further examined the relationship between school demographics and levels of compassion satisfaction and fatigue by performing correlation and linear regression analyses.

For the qualitative component, interviews were transcribed and scrutinized through open coding techniques and literature-informed codes pertinent to compassion fatigue. From these codes, emerging themes were mapped out, and their frequencies within the transcripts were quantified. As a final step, quotes were gathered to illustrate themes.

Sample Pool

The sample pool contained 100 participant teachers. The optional demographic survey yielded additional information about the characteristics of the teachers' schools. See Table 3.1.

TABLE 3.1 Teacher and School Demographic Characteristics

Teaching position	◆ Elementary school – 35% ◆ Middle school – 24% ◆ High school – 37% ◆ Two or more levels – 4%
Teacher ethnicity	◆ African American – 9% ◆ Asian/Pacific Islander – 10% ◆ White – 57% ◆ Hispanic/Latino – 9% ◆ Two or more races – 12% ◆ Prefer not to say – 3%
Gender identity	◆ Female – 78% ◆ Male – 19% ◆ Non-binary – 1% ◆ Prefer not to say – 2%
Age range	◆ 18–35 years – 28% ◆ 36 years and up – 70% ◆ Prefer not to say – 2%
Average number of years in the profession	◆ Fewer than five years – 18% ◆ Five years or more – 82%
Average number of years at the school site	◆ Fewer than five years – 46.9% ◆ Five years or more – 53.1%
% of English learners (ELs) at schools	◆ ELs over 20% – 60% at schools ◆ ELs under 20% – 39.6% at schools
Socioeconomically disadvantaged (SED) status of schools	◆ SED over 70% – 58% of schools ◆ SED under 70% – 42% of schools ◆ Average SED of schools – 71%
Average enrollment by ethnicity and student group	◆ African American (AA) – 11% ◆ Asian Pacific Islander and Filipino (APIF) – 19% ◆ Hispanic/Latino (HL) – 46% ◆ White – 18% ◆ Students with Disabilities (SWD) – 12% ◆ English Learners (EL) – 24%

Quantitative Results of Study 1

Table 3.2 provides a summary of the average PROQOL 5 scores by key demographics discussed in this chapter.

TABLE 3.2 Average (Mean) ProQOL 5 Scores by Sample Demographics

		CS	BO	STS
Female	Mean	50.65	49.59	50.30
	N	78.00	78.00	78.00
	SD	10.35	10.28	9.66
Male	Mean	48.19	50.48	47.66
	N	19.00	19.00	19.00
	SD	7.79	8.40	9.80
Non-binary	Mean	44.56	57.73	57.11
	N	3.00	3.00	3.00
	SD	13.64	12.20	18.94
Percentage of change (female/male)		5%	−2%	5%
Socioeconomically disadvantaged status <70%	Mean	51.15	47.23	48.69
	N	40.00	40.00	40.00
	SD	9.61	8.79	8.45
Socioeconomically disadvantaged status > 70%	Mean	49.69	51.43	51.44
	N	56.00	56.00	56.00
	SD	10.31	10.51	10.99
Percentage of change		−3%	8%	5%
Percentage of English learners < 20%	Mean	50.40	49.38	50.31
	n	38.00	38.00	38.00
	SD	9.14	8.78	10.49
Percentage of English learners > 20%	Mean	50.23	49.87	50.28
	n	58.00	58.00	58.00
	SD	10.60	10.80	9.85
Percentage of change		0%	1%	0%
Teaching < five years	Mean	49.11	50.95	50.98
	n	18.00	18.00	18.00
	SD	7.50	9.49	9.82
Teaching > five years	Mean	50.19	49.79	49.78
	n	82.00	82.00	82.00
	SD	10.50	10.15	10.09
Percentage of change		2%	−2%	−2%

*n means n size; SD means standard deviation.

Teachers Suffer from Compassion Fatigue ♦ 57

♦ *Finding 1 – Female teachers experienced higher CS, lower BO, and higher STS than male teachers while male teachers experienced higher BO than female teachers.*

• On average, female teachers had higher scores on CS (approximately 5% higher) and STS (approximately 5% higher) than male teachers. However, female teachers scored slightly lower on BO (approximately 2% lower) than male teachers. Though the sample of non-binary teachers was very small it is worth noting that non-binary teachers experienced lower CS, higher BO, and higher STS than both male and female teachers. See Figure 3.1.

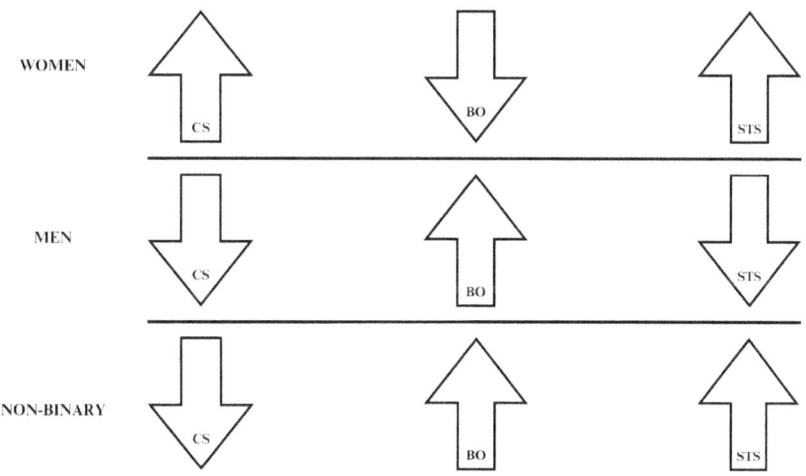

FIGURE 3.1 CS-BO-STS Comparison by Gender Identity

♦ *Finding 2 – Compassion Fatigue appears to be more acute among beginning teachers than with veteran teachers.*

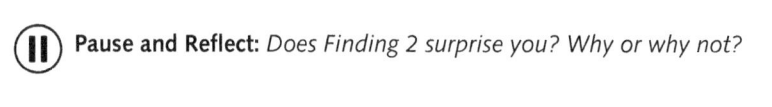

Pause and Reflect: *Does Finding 2 surprise you? Why or why not?*

• Teachers with less than five years of experience in the teaching profession experienced higher BO, higher

58 ♦ Addressing Compassion Fatigue in Urban Schools

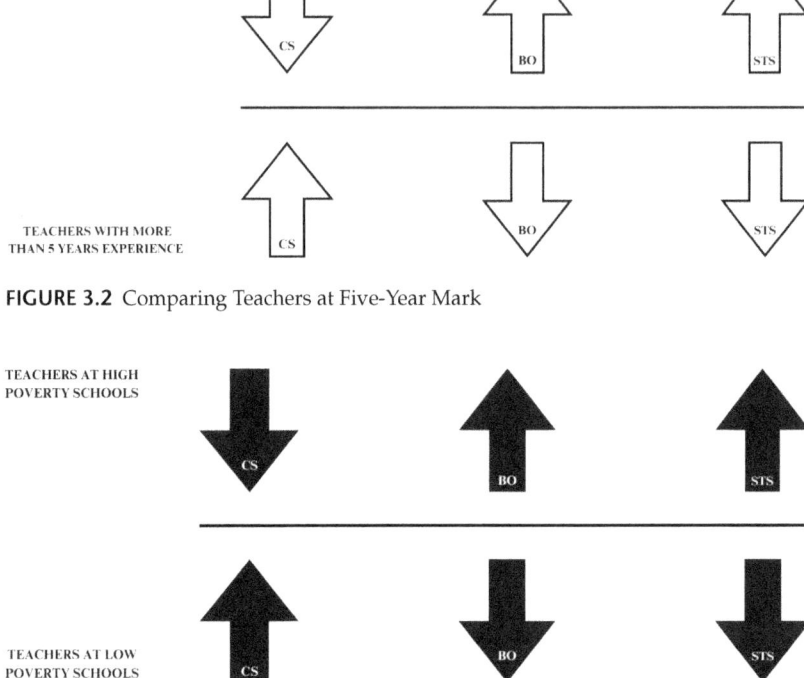

FIGURE 3.2 Comparing Teachers at Five-Year Mark

FIGURE 3.3 High- and Low-Poverty School Comparison

STS, and less CS than teachers with more than five years of experience. See Figure 3.2.

♦ *Finding 3 – Teachers working in high-poverty schools face striking disparities in their levels of compassion satisfaction and fatigue compared to their counterparts in low-poverty schools.*

• The data reveal statistically significant differences, with teachers in high-poverty schools showing statistically significantly lower levels of compassion satisfaction, higher rates of burnout, and significantly elevated levels of secondary traumatic stress. See Figure 3.3.

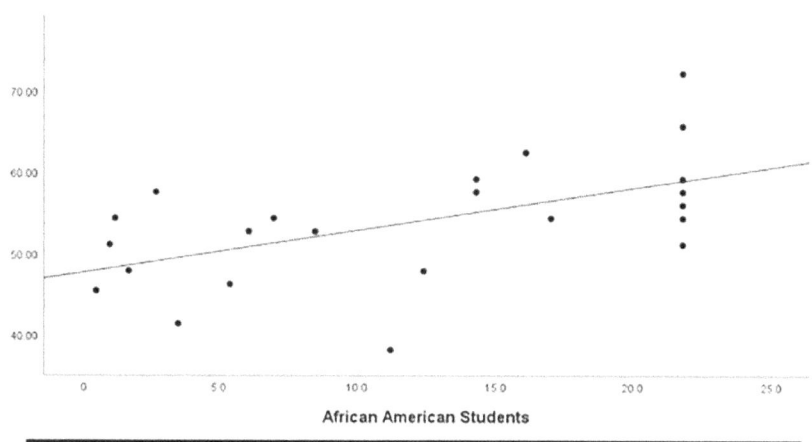

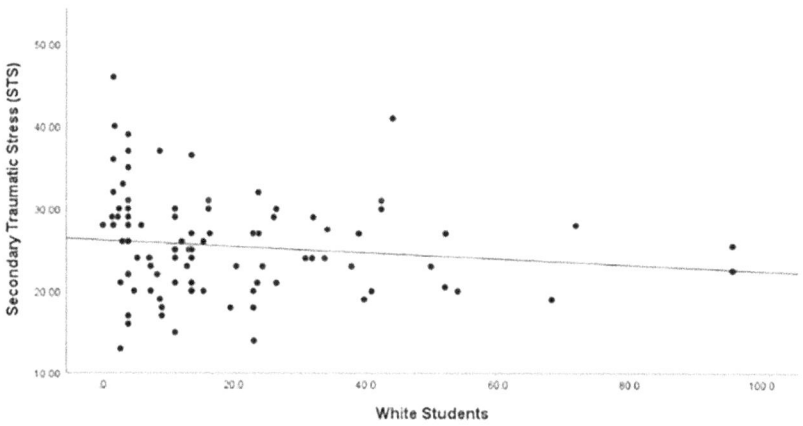

FIGURE 3.4 Teachers' STS t-score vs. African American and White student Count

- *Finding 4 – Correlation tests revealed statistically significant relationships between compassion fatigue and the school's demographics.*
  - In particular, the mix of African American and White students in a school significantly predicted compassion fatigue among teachers. Linear regression

models demonstrated that the percentage of African American students in the school was a statistically significant predictor of compassion fatigue (burnout and secondary traumatic stress scores) for teachers. As the percentage of African American students increases, secondary traumatic stress and burnout scores also tend to increase, which is illustrated in Figure 3.4.

♦ Conversely, at the middle school level, there is a statistically significant correlation between the percentage of White students in the school and compassion satisfaction and fatigue. As the school's percentage of White students increases so do compassion satisfaction scores, burnout, and secondary traumatic stress score decline. Additionally, at the middle school level, a school's socioeconomic disadvantage status significantly influences a teacher's compassion satisfaction and burnout scores.

One Final Note on Quantitative Results

The data and analysis consistently showed statistically significant relationships between various student and teacher demographic factors and teacher well-being (compassion satisfaction, burnout, secondary traumatic stress) at the middle school level even when controlling for poverty and teacher ethnicity. Ultimately showing that the effects of student racial composition and socioeconomic factors on teacher well-being are strong enough to remain significant even when considering teacher ethnicity, poverty, and years in the profession. The socioeconomically disadvantaged status of the school consistently emerged as a significant predictor of teacher well-being, affecting compassion satisfaction, burnout, and secondary traumatic stress. The racial composition of students, particularly the percentages of African American and White students, played a role in predicting teacher well-being, with different impacts on compassion satisfaction, burnout, and secondary traumatic stress. A teacher's years of experience, both in the profession and at the school site, show correlations with well-being, particularly for less experienced teachers.

Overall, the findings suggest that compassion fatigue in teachers and their professional well-being and quality of life is influenced by a combination of factors, including school site demographics, student racial groups, teacher demographics, and teacher experience.

Pause and Reflect: *Why do you think a statistically significant relationship exists between a teacher's compassion satisfaction and fatigue scores and a student's race?*

Qualitative Results of Study 1

Follow-up interviews with teacher participants further illuminated areas of concern. A total of six interviews were conducted with educators who took the ProQOL 5. These interviews included three middle school teachers (Adam, Alex, and Abby), two high school teachers (Alan and Amy), and one elementary school teacher (Alice). Please note that names were changed to protect privacy. The interviews were transcribed, analyzed, and coded to identify common themes. Selected portions of the interviews were then transformed into illustrative stories called vignettes. These vignettes serve to both convey the experiences of each teacher and highlight the key themes that emerged from the interviews. Notably, Adam retired at the end of the school year, while Alan and Abby transitioned to different schools. Alex and Alice remained at their current school, and Amy expressed her intention to retire in the near future.

A Summary of Teachers' Experiences
Compassion Satisfaction

Teachers found their greatest satisfaction in their relationships with colleagues, which they regarded as a vital source of support. For example, Alice credited her teacher colleagues as the reason she continued teaching after a particularly challenging experience. She expressed, "I have a group of teachers that they're like my family. And they did support me. And they got me through it." Many teachers mentioned that discussing their concerns with coworkers helped them process difficult situations and provided comfort during moments of stress caused by students' behavior or life circumstances.

Burnout

Teachers grappling with burnout described various distressing characteristics that left them feeling irritable and moody toward students, colleagues, and family members. They often attributed these difficulties to factors such as students' behavior, negative interactions with parents of students, school administration, and even self-blame. Some teachers expressed cynicism about the potential for improvement in student behavior and believed that students lacked the social capital needed for success, primarily attributing this to students' parents. Constantly compensating for this lack of social capital took a toll on their physical and mental well-being. For example, Alex shared an instance when he struggled to engage a student due to unresponsive parents, resulting in troubling classroom disruptions.

Secondary Trauma

Teachers also experienced secondary trauma, feeling depressed or saddened by their students' traumatic experiences and interactions. Many described a profound sense of hopelessness and the inability to prevent distressing situations from occupying their minds after work hours. For instance, Adam recounted an incident where he felt disheartened by his inability to help a student who had been molested, triggering memories of his own childhood sexual trauma, which resulted in Adam suffering a mental breakdown in the middle of the school year. To cope he taught himself to detach personally from the student and not to care as much. Adam describes how he came to this realization in this way:

> *I remember [what I] learned around that event…I remember talking to the other science teacher at the school about that girl. I think I even broke down crying talking to her, and she just said you can't save every one of them. You're going to have to learn that. And I mean that was a real valuable thing for her*

> *to tell me—that I just can't. You know as a teacher, as someone who suffered from the same kind of things that they [students] do, I want to but...the funny thing is, the realization I had is to think about myself!*
>
> (Ollison, 2019a, pp. 121–122)

Distancing himself emotionally from students became a major coping strategy for Adam.

Unfortunately, suicide was also a common traumatic experience teachers faced, except for elementary school teacher Alice. These experiences often left teachers in a state of emotional distress. Abby shared her profound experiences with student suicides and the emotional toll it took on her, especially in the absence of proper training in suicide prevention. Her first experience with suicide occurred in her second year of teaching:

> *I think my second year there, there was a student I'd had for seventh and eighth grade and he did go home and commit suicide one day and that really affected me. So, whenever it [suicide] comes up it's like a really dark part for me to think back to that, because at the time there was no teacher care. There was no, "hey how are you feeling? you want to talk about this?" It was just like [they] give someone else a seat because everyone needs to sit down. And we just moved on and I was new in the profession.*
>
> (Ollison, 2019a, p. 122)

Abby then went on to describe three more experiences with students or the siblings of students committing suicide. She described that the suicides were very hard on her because she was not trained in suicide prevention and therefore unequipped to handle the aftereffects for herself or her students. She described herself as being in a "strange emotional position" that did not get better until she went through a mental health first aid certification training that discussed secondary traumatic stress and educator self-care. She shared that the trainers helped her talk through her experience, "they gave me a name they gave me a name for it. So, I felt less crazed" (Ollison, 2019a, p. 122).

School Conditions and Climate

Teachers frequently discussed the character and quality of their school's environment, emphasizing the importance of values, expectations, interpersonal relationships, critical resources, support, and practices. They expressed concerns about how the actions of various actors in the school, including parents, students, fellow teachers, and administrators, influenced their ability to create safe and academically challenging environments. Teachers often found their morale affected by how students were treated by the system and how students treated them. This included concerns about the availability of basic supplies, the poor condition of facilities like bathrooms, and the lack of appreciation from school administrators. For instance, Amy mentioned feeling unappreciated at her school, which contributed to her sense of burnout. Alex described teaching at his school as an ongoing battle, highlighting the challenges of helping students from disadvantaged backgrounds and maintaining his own energy levels to meet his teaching expectations. This characterization underscored the importance of fostering a supportive and inclusive school environment to alleviate the challenges teachers face.

Teachers Experience with Various Types of Traumas and Their Responses to It

The interviews brought to light numerous traumatic experiences that teachers experienced. I think it is important to share them here so that you can get a clear picture of what teachers are dealing with on a daily basis and can understand why it is so important that efforts to mitigate teacher composition fatigue be undertaken immediately. These traumas are categorized into three distinct types: student-based, parent-based, and working conditions-based.

Student-Based Trauma

This refers to secondary trauma experienced by teachers as a direct result of the trauma their students endure. It arises from their close exposure to the emotional and psychological struggles faced by students, which in turn affects the well-being of teachers.

These experiences included neglect, child abuse, divorce of students' parents, child molestation, difficult home environments, student suicides and suicide attempts, sexual assault, and more. Teachers often had to act as makeshift therapists for students in distress despite lacking proper training.

Parent-Based Trauma

This type of trauma stems from challenging and distressing encounters or interactions with parents of students. These interactions can be emotionally taxing and have a lasting impact on teachers. This included being threatened by parents over the phone, facing verbal and professional attacks in front of school administration, and experiencing the mishandling of parent complaints, which resulted in unfair treatment, anxiety, and humiliation.

Working Conditions-Based Trauma

This trauma arises from specific school-related factors, such as the overall working environment, school climate, and the relationship with school and district administration. It encompasses challenges related to school conditions, policies, and the general atmosphere that teachers must navigate. Teachers faced issues such as students lacking basic supplies, broken furniture, lack of air conditioning, malfunctioning student bathrooms, lack of support from administration, excessive workloads (especially for special education teachers), exclusion from important conversations about student support, and lack of staff debriefings after traumatic events involving students.

The Teachers Described a Range of Reactions to Trauma

Here is a summary of those described reactions below.

- ♦ **Emotional Responses:** Teachers experienced emotional pain, sadness, and fear for their students' well-being. Some could relate their own backgrounds to their students' trauma, which was emotionally taxing. Others experienced irritability and found themselves snapping at their own families or loved ones.

- **Compartmentalization:** Teachers often had to separate their personal emotions from their students' trauma to be present for them, even when the situations were distressing.

- **Negative Attitudes:** Some teachers adopted negative attitudes toward school administration, feeling that administrators did not truly understand the challenges they faced in the classroom.

- **Reduced Compassion:** Over time, some teachers became less compassionate toward students who externalized their pain from trauma.

- **Coping Strategies:** Teachers employed various coping mechanisms, such as convincing themselves that they couldn't save everyone, numbing their emotions, and taking "mental health" days off from work.

- **Dealing with Problem Students:** Teachers resorted to constantly sending problem students to the office with referrals in the hope that the administration would act.

- **Impact on Well-being:** Traumatic experiences led to feelings of being unsupported, discouraged with colleagues and the school community, and a desire to quit or take time off from work. Some even requested reduced workloads, took excessive amounts of days off, retired, or left their schools due to the impact of trauma.

- **Physical and Mental Health Effects:** Teachers experienced physical exhaustion, sleepless nights, crying both at home and at school, and symptoms such as nervous breakdowns, avoiding students and parents in public, mental breakdowns, burnout, depression, anxiety, irritability, and hyperventilation.

- **Personal Triggers:** Some traumatic experiences triggered teachers' personal memories or past experiences, further exacerbating their distress.

FIGURE 3.5 Emotional Progression

 Pause and Reflect: *A range of teachers' emotions and reactions to trauma were described. Have you experienced any of the emotions or reactions to trauma described here? If so, what?*

Summary of Qualitative Themes

The themes and subthemes extracted from the interviews reflect the sentiments shared by teachers on a deeper level. These themes capture not only explicit feelings but also the underlying ideas that shape these sentiments. Throughout the interviews, a common thread was the recognition, or sometimes the lack thereof, that every member of the school community – teachers, administrators, students, and parents – are a part of the school and school system; all are impacted by system stressors. These themes consider the inherent challenges of the teaching profession, which are further complicated by societal factors like poverty, race, and trauma.

Theme 1 – Teachers Experience Secondary Trauma

This theme delves into the profound impact of secondary trauma on teachers. Teachers described how this secondary trauma affected them on both personal and professional levels. They recounted experiences of mental, physical, and emotional stress that made it challenging for them to effectively teach.

Theme 1 Subthemes

- *Profound Effect of Student Suicide:*
  - Within this theme, one subtheme revolves around the devastating impact of student suicide on teachers. Teachers shared emotional stories of how the loss of a student to suicide deeply affected them and their teaching experiences.

- *Secondary Trauma Impedes Teacher Self-Efficacy:*
  - This subtheme highlights how the secondary trauma experienced by teachers could hinder their sense of self-efficacy. Teachers discussed how their own emotional struggles and empathy for their students' trauma sometimes made it difficult for them to be as effective in the classroom as they wanted to be.

- *Teachers' Lives Outside of School Cause Stress Too:*
  - Another subtheme is the recognition that teachers have lives outside of school, and these personal challenges can add to their stress. Teachers shared experiences of dealing with personal issues such as family illnesses and friends' difficulties, which compounded their stress and affected their teaching.

Theme 2 – Secondary Trauma Is Not the Only Trauma Teachers Experience

This theme highlights that teachers face various forms of trauma beyond just secondary trauma from their students. It underscores that school conditions and climate, interactions with parents, and decisions made by school administrators also contribute to teacher stress and trauma.

Theme 2 Subthemes

- *School Administrators Do Not Always Understand Teacher's Everyday Classroom Experience:*

- A significant subtheme in this category is the feeling of not being fully supported by school administrators. Teachers expressed that school administrators often did not grasp the day-to-day challenges they faced in the classroom, leading to a sense of disconnect.

- *Concerns about Trauma Caused by Parent Interaction:*
  - Another subtheme is the challenges associated with parent interactions. Teachers shared stories of feeling blamed or unsupported by parents, which created additional stress and contributed to their trauma.

- *Concerns about Trauma Caused by Exacerbation of Working Conditions:*
  - Teachers also discussed how administrative decisions related to teaching assignments, workload, student discipline, staff discipline, parent interactions, and supplies could exacerbate working conditions. These decisions often led to heightened stress levels among teachers.

Theme 3 – It Is Easier to Have Compassion for Students Who Are Easier to Handle Than Others

This theme explores the complexities of managing student behavior and the toll it takes on teachers' capacity for compassion. Teachers described how dealing with students exhibiting disruptive or challenging behavior drained their emotional energy and made it difficult to maintain empathy.

Theme 3 Subthemes:

- *Challenges of Student Behavior:*
  - A central subtheme revolves around the difficulties teachers face in managing student behavior. Teachers shared stories of students who exhibited disruptive, disrespectful, or defiant behavior, which presented significant challenges to maintaining a positive classroom environment and positive attitude towards students.

- ♦ *Blame and Teacher-Student Relationships:*
  - Teachers often expressed a sense of blame directed at students, teachers themselves, and administration for the disruptive behavior. This theme suggests that the prevalence of challenging student behavior can lead to a breakdown in teacher-student relationships.

- ♦ *Impact on Teacher's Personal Life:*
  - This theme also delves into how the stress and emotional toll from managing challenging student behavior can spill over into teachers' personal lives, contributing to their overall stress and well-being.

Theme 4 – I Still Have a Job to Do

This theme underscores the unwavering commitment of teachers to their duty of ensuring students' learning, even in the face of distressing events, trauma, and disruptive behavior. Teachers often held themselves responsible for meeting this obligation, leading to feelings of guilt, inadequacy, and self-perceived failure.

Theme 4 Subthemes

- ♦ *Feelings of Guilt and Inadequacy:*
  - Teachers expressed a deep sense of guilt and inadequacy when they felt they were not meeting their obligation to ensure student learning. These feelings often stemmed from the challenging circumstances they faced in their classrooms.

- ♦ *Self-Care and Career Decisions:*
  - Some teachers chose to take self-care measures, such as taking time off or transferring to a different school, as a response to the stress and challenges they encountered. These decisions were made with the awareness that they needed to prioritize their well-being to be effective educators.

Theme 5 – Teachers Have Conscious and Unconscious Biases Toward an Ideal Type of Student

This theme delves into the biases that teachers hold regarding an ideal student. An ideal student is often perceived as respectful, academically inclined, and potentially in need of additional support due to challenging life circumstances. While the theme doesn't explicitly mention the role of race in these perceptions, it suggests that teachers' perceptions of school climate can be influenced by students' race and behavior.

Theme 5 Subthemes

- *Ideal Student Characteristics:*
  - Teachers tend to have a vision of an ideal student who is respectful, engaged, and eager to learn. This vision often guides their perceptions of students and school climate. That is, anyone who doesn't fit this mold is seen as challenging and difficult.

- *Influence of Student Demographics:*
  - While not explicitly stated in the theme, it's implied that the demographics of students, including their race and behavior, can influence teachers' perceptions of school climate. Teachers mentioned feeling more challenged when dealing with African American students and parents. This underscores the need for more culturally responsive training for educators.

- *Impact on Teacher Well-Being:*
  - This theme also suggests that the dynamics between teachers and students, particularly when dealing with challenging behavior, can have a significant impact on teachers' overall well-being and job satisfaction.

I Blame Student Behavior

Meghan, Middle School Special Education Teacher

I am not saying it is all bad but sometimes students' behavior is so awful I dread going to school. In fact, before I came to this school, which is a breath of fresh air by the way, students' behavior was so bad I literally couldn't teach and my students couldn't learn. It wasn't just my classroom though; it was the whole school. For example, we had three fights in the first week of school. A teacher who tried to break one up was pushed and dared by the student to do anything. There were threats of violence made on social media that caused more police presence on campus. In my classroom I had one student whose behavior ran hot and cold. One day he was awesome and the next he was a nightmare. He had physically attacked students and me. Once it took two teachers to get him off me. The staff used to talk about the need for change. That safety was an issue and that more people were going to keep leaving or taking FMLA if something wasn't done. Ultimately, I did leave the school – not the profession. I am much happier now at a charter school. I feel safe every day now and my stress level has gone way down.

 Pause and Reflect: *Does Meghan's story resonate with you? Why or why not?*

Summing Up Study 1

In summary, this study shows that secondary trauma from students is not the only trauma teachers are experiencing. Trauma is school conditions and climate based and parents or school site administration sometimes cause it. Common threads among all interviews were the implication that school administrators do not always understand the teacher's everyday classroom experience and that parents sometimes feel like enemies, even though they are not supposed to be.

The obligation and duty felt to ensure students are learning the curriculum, which is always foremost in the mind of the teacher, *and they feel guilty when the obligation is not met*. The guilt is compounded by teachers struggle with knowing that it is easier to have compassion for students who are easier to handle than others. Often, the students are so challenging that it inhibits the teacher's desire to engage with the student, let alone teach them. What's more the perception of these students, all students, factors into the teacher's perceptions of the school's climate – sometimes for the worse.

The character and quality of the school (Collie et al., 2012, p. 1191) and the values, expectations, interpersonal relationships, critical resources, supports, and practices that foster or inhibit a welcoming, inclusive, and academically challenging environment are extremely important. That is, **school climate and conditions matter.** Teachers have concerns about how actions taken by school environment actors including parents, students, other teachers, and administrators affect their ability to create safe and academically challenging environments. Teacher morale is often affected by how students are treated or how students are treating them.

The data in this study highlight the complex challenges teachers face in managing their own trauma, navigating student behavior, and maintaining their commitment to education. The data illustrate the profound impact of trauma on teachers' well-being and their ability to effectively teach and support their students. It underscores the need for comprehensive support systems and strategies to address the emotional toll that teaching in challenging environments can take on educators. For example, **all teachers should be certified in mental health first aid training with a focus on children and adolescents.** From a policy perspective, it should be just as important as regular first aid training. The context of the world we live in makes having this type of training a necessity for teachers and the students they serve, and the absence of it is tantamount to educational malpractice. However, in the absence of systemwide changes in support of teachers and their training – it will be incumbent on the teacher to take up the charge for themselves and do what is necessary to ensure they are equipped for success.

Navigating the Complexities

Understanding these complexities felt like a moral imperative for me. It led me to make a compassionate plea for all to see via a TEDx talk entitled: Compassion Fatigue: Teachers Are Suffering and It Impacts All of Us (Ollison, 2019b). It also led to workshops and professional development training opportunities, but it wasn't enough as the idea was slow to spread. And then the pandemic hit, and March 2020 saw the massive closure of business and schools across the country. Suddenly we were thrust into an unfamiliar world wrought with sickness and death that many of this generation have never experienced. How were we to deal with it? How were we to tackle schooling considering it? Educators – district and state leadership, administrators, teachers, and classified staff – frantically produced plans to ensure students' education continued even if just remotely. But time and time again, systemwide issues made it difficult. The lack of internet access, lack of technology, and lack of digital literacy on the part of educators who had to teach remotely, and the seeming disappearance of hundreds of students got in the way of operating schools the way they had always been operated (Stelitano et al. (n.d.); Golden et al., 2023).

People were realizing just how important teachers are for the proper functioning of the country. One can't go to work if they don't have someone to watch their children, and schools are essentially free childcare especially when before-and-after-school programs are a part of the school day. In addition, the approximately 60% of children receiving nutritious breakfast and lunch at school for free (California Department of Education [Data Reporting Office], n.d.) were no longer receiving them.

At same time, we were also dealing with massive amounts of death which disproportionately impacted Black and Indigenous populations, the elderly and medically vulnerable populations (J. Moore et al., 2020; Yancy, 2020). People lost their jobs. Protective equipment for essential workers was hard to come by and so were eggs and toilet paper (Ranney et al., 2020). It was a lot. And for children, especially high-poverty students, COVID had a disproportionate impact on the wealth and mortality of their family members (J. Moore et al., 2020; Yancy, 2020).

Synopsis of Second Study: 2021–2022

I wondered whether there was a pandemic-influenced impact on teachers' experiences with compassion fatigue, which is where the second study comes in. The sample size in this study was 67 participants. It included 13 administrators and 54 teachers. And while this book focuses on teachers, the experiences of administrators is relevant in that it illuminates the experience of teachers and leaders in the system and can thus lead to more comprehensive understanding of what teachers were dealing with personally and professionally. The majority of the sample, 62, had over five years of teaching experience. There were very few statistically significant relationships observed, and thus I will not discuss them here, but what I do want to share was eye opening especially given that this was conducted during the 2021–2022 school year, at the height of the COVID-19 pandemic. Here is what I learned.

Quantitative Results of Study 1

Across the board most participants scored in the high range for CS, BO, and STS. See Table 3.3.

Stamm (2010) describes compassion fatigue score ranges as follows 22 or less is low, between 23 and 41 is moderate, and 42 or more is high. As you can see in Table 3.3, there was only one score that fell in the low range for both CS and BO and no low scores for STS at all. What's more, there were high levels of BO and STS observed, and this is very concerning because the combination of high levels of burnout and secondary traumatic stress are extremely worrisome. According to Stamm (2010), this combination may indicate that someone is feeling very overwhelmed by their work setting and that they find it quite frightening. Stamm (2010) further argues that people with scores like this could benefit from leaving their work setting. No statistically significant differences in scores were noted between high- and low-poverty schools as in the first study. See Figure 3.6.

What is interesting here is that compassion satisfaction is also high. What this may reflect is that during the pandemic teachers and administrators derived satisfaction from their work in education. It is likely that they felt like they were making a positive difference in the lives of students at that time and there was some professional

TABLE 3.3 CS, BO, and STS Score Ranges and Means

Scores Range	# High	Average	# Moderate	Average	# Low	Average
CS range	57	52.70	9	36.72	1	15.48
BO range	52	53.96	14	37.48	1	19.41
STS range	54	53.11	13	37.09	N/A	N/A

FIGURE 3.6 Compassion Satisfaction and Fatigue Score Range

fulfillment because of that. This is interesting because the previous study did not show such high levels of compassion satisfaction.

Qualitative Results of Study 2

Similarly, to the first study, interviews revealed the types of pandemic-influenced experiences with compassion fatigue educators were dealing with and how they coped. Here is a brief synopsis of the findings.

The Pandemic Had a Profound Impact on Their Compassion Fatigue and Perceptions of School Climate

Educators relayed a variety of unpleasant experiences that impacted their ability to function optimally which are summarized as follows:

- *Overwhelm and Burnout*
  - Educators experienced high levels of stress, questioning their purpose, and feeling burned out due to increased workloads and emotional burdens. The transition from teaching in-person to online was difficult for some. They found that they were not prepared, and neither were their students. They also expressed that returning to work during the OMICRON resurgence of COVID was difficult (Gewertz, 2022). Teachers were worried about their health and the health of their families, as were students. There also seemed to be more work not less, with the preparing of students for state testing taking precendence even though the prior chool years learning did not go well. Teachers also described that induction demands, before-and-after-school tutoring, and the additional work led to feelings of overwhelm.

- *Student Disengagement*
  - Teachers observed that students have become more apathetic since the pandemic, affecting their motivation and participation, which in turn impacts the teachers' ability to create an engaging climate. One teacher indicated that she stopped assigning homework because students weren't doing it, she also allowed for more time to complete assignments, but approximately 70% of her students had a C or below grade. This was also noted in the interview's with administrators. Many students experienced trauma and loss of loved ones, homes, and financial stability. In addition, the online year of schooling led to poor study habits and coping mechanisms in students. Once they returned to campus the ability to cope with "productive struggle"was not there and many students gave up. Unfortunately so did the teachers as evidence by the decisions to not assign homework because students were not completing it.

- *Challenges with Student Behavior and Trauma*
  - Administrators noted that there was a notable increase in behavioral issues and trauma-related incidents among students, which impacted thierthe ability to maintain a beneficial learning environment. For example, one administrator shared that he used to have good relationships with the students who were seen frequently in the office and now those same students cuss him out. There was also an increase in drug usage and chronic absenteeism. Chronic absenteeism was also phenomenon observed statewide, as "chronic absence rates increased from 12 percent (702,531 students) in 2018–19 to a high of 30 percent (1,799,734) in 2021–22" (Chang et al., 2024).

- *Resource Stretching, Increased Demands, and Stress*
  - Administrators felt as though they did nothave enough support or resources to assist all students effectively, particularly special education students. There was lso a lack of support when it came to staffing as it was

difficult to find classified staff to fill vital roles like classroom aides, bus drivers, campus security, and cafeteria workers. This led to administrators having to wear multiple hats as they tackled the overwhelming demands from their job roles, leading to emotional exhaustion and a lack of personal time, and less ability to offer support to teachers.

- ♦ *Empathy Overload*
  - Additionally, administrators suffered from empathy overload. They were deeply affected by the personal struggles of families and students, and teachers leading to a high emotional burden, tears, numbing behavior, and sadness. Both administrators and teachers struggled with compassion fatigue during the pandemic. One administrator described how she went to great lengths to ensure staff remained connected while they were virtual, but that connection was not the same once they returned to in-person schooling. Once, she was accused of taking a vacation when she missed two weeks of school due to contracting COVID.

- ♦ *Coping Behaviors to Combat Compassion Fatigue*
  - When asked what coping behaviors they utilized to combat the effects of pandemic-influenced compassion fatigue, they shared the following:

- ♦ *Boundary Setting*
  - Some educators set clear boundaries to prevent burnout, such as cutting back on after-hours work and keeping a work-life balance by returning to activities they found enjoyable.

- ♦ *Seeking Professional Help*
  - Some teachers resorted to therapy and medication to cope with anxiety and depression.

- *Self-Care*
  - Some tried engaging in activities like exercise, baking, or "procrastibaking". One teacher explained that the coping mechanism was **more of a distraction** from dealing with the demands of thierwork and life, then it was self-care, or hobbies designed to relieve stress and maintain personal well-being.

- *Emotional Detachment*
  - Some administrators tried to distance themselves from the emotions that they were feeling at work and at home. For example, they delayed responses to emails and voicemail as a way to manage overwhelming communications. They also set boundaries because the work never seemed to stop. One administrator even shared, "there are no boundaries anymore – assistant superintendents, superintendents and the board – are communicating on Friday at 8 pm or Sunday night."

- *Seeking Emotional Support*
  - Some did find solace in conversations with trusted colleagues or friends to discuss the stress and emotional pain of the work.

- *Consideration of Career Change or Break*
  - And once again it was observed that stress led some participants to contemplate taking a break or changing their career path.

Impact on Educators' Perception of School Climate and Working Conditions

It is clear that the pandemic affected teachers and their school leaders. What is particularly concerning is the impact it had on how they perceived the school's climate and working conditions. The strain of the pandemic changed how some teachers view their profession for the worse, with some considering early retirement or career changes due to the stressful environment. Remember, positive school climates aren't just for students they are for adults too

(Kraft & Falken, 2020; Rubinstein & McCarthy, 2016). And working conditions continue to be cited as a major reason why educators leave the profession (Mathews & Hart Research Associates, 2022).

> *Pause and Reflect: Did you find teaching during the pandemic more challenging than before the pandemic? Why or why not? Have things improved for you?*

Summing Up Study 2

The need for more support was prevalent, especially since many felt unsupported by the system. Educators expressed a desire for more aid in the classroom, more school site staff, and better compensation to ensure they could hire support staff to deal with the increased challenges. Dynamics within schools were evolving, with educators reporting more strained or altered relationships with students, parents, and staff due to the ongoing pandemic. Administrators indicated that they felt like "punching bags" as they had to bear the brunt of parents, staff, and public ire as they navigated pandemic challenges such as on-and-off again mask mandates and in person versus online schooling. What's more troubling is that teachers felt like there should have been more grace for educators, given how at the beginning of the pandemic teachers were sorely missed by parents and thus more valued.

But as they returned to school so did the disdain for teachers. Some felt a pervasive sense of inadequacy as they struggled to meet the diverse needs of their students despite their efforts. And lastly, empathy and compassion for apathetic students waned. Given the seriousness of the trauma COVID caused for students and educators, waning empathy is not ideal nor what the school system needs. When combined with the quantitative results, I take these findings to mean that even though educators found fulfillment in their jobs it was "literally" burning and stressing them out. And both of these studies showed that this is not sustainable for the teaching profession.

Teaching is a people's job. Teachers interact with individuals daily. Students deserve adults who are healthy physically, mentally, and emotionally. Castro et al. (2023) argue that teacher morale is declining due to contextual factors like the loss of autonomy due to things like restrictive legislation, particularly regarding race-related topics, stress, teacher shortages, and the COVID-19 pandemic. When one is suffering from compassion fatigue or high burnout and secondary traumatic stress, they are much more likely to be irritable, moody, apathetic, negative, detached, socially withdrawn from students and colleagues, unable to get along well with colleagues, and absent physically and to suffer from low morale just to name a few (Kyer, 2020). This sounds a lot like the teaching profession right now (Castro et al., 2023; Mathews & Hart Research Associates, 2022). And it is definitely not an environment that school aged children should be subjected to.

I know that the research presented here showed some scary results. In fact, I bet you might even be feeling upset, just like I was when I first studied it. Truthfully, I was also happy about the results. I felt vindicated. For a long time, I felt conflicted about my teaching and leading experiences. Especially the negative ones. But this research made the participants feel seen, understood, and less alone. I took comfort in knowing that it showed that even though teachers might feel as if they are the only one experiencing burnout, secondary trauma, and a range of conflicting emotions they are not. YOU ARE NOT ALONE. There is hope. There are things you can do to feel better. In the next chapter I offer recommendations for action based on this research aimed at combating compassion fatigue in teachers.

 Connect the Thoughts

1. What feelings or insights do you have about the research presented in this chapter?
2. Describe a time when you may have experienced compassion fatigue: burnout, or secondary trauma, both in your work or personal life.
3. Did the pandemic affect your experiences with which is compassion fatigue? If so, how?

4. What connections do you see to your school site or school district?
5. Do you feel less alone? Why or why not?

References

Borkowski, A., Ortiz Correa, J. S., Bundy, D. A. P., Burbano, C., Hayashi, C., Lloyd-Evans, E., Neitzel, J., & Reuge, N. (2021). *The impact of school closures on children's nutrition COVID – Missing more than a classroom.* UNICEF Innocenti Research Centre. Retrieved February 3, 2024, from https://www.unicef-irc.org

California Department of Education [Data Reporting Office]. (n.d.). *Student poverty free and reduced price meals data.* Dataquest. Retrieved January 13, 2024, from https://tinyurl.com/3un4522e

Castro, A. J., Edmondson, E., & Santoro, D. A. (2023). Shifting the gaze: Examining contextual factors influencing teacher morale in suburban schools. *American Journal of Education*, *130*(1), 61–87. https://doi.org/10.1086/727008

Chang, H., Chavez, B., & Hough, H. J. (2024, January 1). *PACE – Unpacking California's chronic absence crisis through 2022–23.* Policy Analysis for California Education. Retrieved February 4, 2024, from https://edpolicyinca.org/publications/unpacking-californias-chronic-absence-crisis-through-2022-23

Cid-Martinez, I., Perez, D., & Marvin, S. (2023, October 19). *The strong labor market recovery has helped Hispanic workers, but the end of economic relief measures has worsened income and poverty disparities.* Economic Policy Institute. Retrieved December 31, 2023, from https://www.epi.org/blog/the-strong-labor-market-recovery-has-helped-hispanic-workers-but-the-end-of-economic-relief-measures-has-worsened-income-and-poverty-disparities/.

Collie, R. J., Shapka, J. D., & Perry, N. E. (2012). School climate and social–emotional learning: Predicting teacher stress, job satisfaction, and teaching efficacy. *Journal of Educational Psychology*, *104*(4), 1189–1204. https://doi.org/10.1037/a0029356

Gewertz, S. S. (2022, January 7). Omicron is making a mess of instruction, even where schools are open. *Education Week.* Retrieved February 3, 2024, from https://www.edweek.org/teaching-learning/omicron-is-making-a-mess-of-instruction-even-where-schools-are-open/ 2022/01

Figley, C. R. (1995). Compassion fatigue as secondary traumatic stress disorder: An overview. In C. R. Figley (Ed.), *Compassion fatigue: Coping with secondary traumatic stress disorder in those who treat the traumatized* (Psychosocial Stress Series) (Vol. 1, pp. 1–18). New York: Brunner/Mazel.

Golden, A. R., Srisarajivakul, E. N., Hasselle, A. J., Pfund, R. A., & Knox, J. (2023). What was a gap is now a chasm: Remote schooling, the digital divide, and educational inequities resulting from the COVID-19 pandemic. *Current Opinion in Psychology*, *52*, 101632. https://doi.org/10.1016/j.copsyc.2023.101632

Herr, K., & Anderson, G. L. (2015). *The action research dissertation: A guide for students and faculty* (2nd ed.) [Kindle]. Thousand Oaks, CA: Sage Publications.

Johnson, R. C. (2023). *School funding effectiveness: Evidence from California's local control funding formula*. Palo Alto, CA: Learning Policy Institute. Retrieved June 25, 2024, from https://doi.org/10.54300/529.194

Johnson, R. B., & Christensen, L. (2016). *Educational research: Quantitative, qualitative, and mixed approaches* (6th ed.). Thousand Oaks, CA: Sage Publications.

Kyer, B. D. (2020). *Surviving compassion fatigue: Help for those who help others*. Cheyenne, WY: Urlink Print & Media, LLC.

Kraft, M. A., & Falken, G. T. (2020, May 18). *Why school climate matters for teachers and students*. Shanker Institute. Retrieved February 4, 2024, from https://www.shankerinstitute.org/blog/why-school-climate-matters-teachers-and-students

Mathews, K., Ph. D. & Hart Research Associates. (2022). *Voices from the classroom: Developing a strategy for teacher retention and recruitment: Key findings from a survey of TK-12 teachers in California and in-depth interviews with aspiring and former teachers in California*. Retrieved February 3, 2024, from https://transformschools.ucla.edu/research/voices-from-the-classroom/.

Moore, K. K. (2022, June 15). *Stratification economics: A moral policy approach for addressing persistent group-based disparities*. Economic Policy Institute. Retrieved December 31, 2023, from https://www.epi.org/publication/stratification-economics/

Moore, J., Ricaldi, J. N., Rose, C. E., Fuld, J., Parise, M. E., Kang, G., Driscoll, A. K., Norris, T., Wilson, N., Rainisch, G., Valverde, E., Beresovsky, V., Brune, C. A., Oussayef, N. L., Rose, D. A., Adams, L., Awel, S., Villanueva, J., Meaney-Delman, D., . . . Westergaard, R. P. (2020). Disparities in incidence of COVID-19 among underrepresented Racial/Ethnic groups in counties identified as hotspots during June 5–18, 2020—22 states, February–June 2020. *Morbidity and Mortality Weekly Report*, *69*(33), 1122–1126. https://doi.org/10.15585/mmwr.mm6933e1

Ollison, J. (2019b, November). *Compassion fatigue: Teachers are suffering, and it impacts all of us* [Video]. TEDxOhloneCollege. Retrieved February 3, 2024, from https://www.youtube.com/watch?v=-Cmc-5sU5L4&feature=youtu.be

Podolsky, A., Kini, T., Bishop, J. B., & Darling-Hammond, L. (2016). *Solving the teacher shortage: How to attract and retain excellent educators*. Retrieved February 3, 2024, from https://doi.org/10.54300/262.960

Ranney, M. L., Griffeth, V., & Jha, A. K. (2020). Critical supply shortages — The need for ventilators and personal protective equipment during the Covid-19 pandemic. *The New England Journal of Medicine*, *382*(18), e41. https://doi.org/10.1056/nejmp2006141

Rubinstein, S. A., & McCarthy, J. E. (2016). Union–management partnerships, teacher collaboration, and student performance. *ILR Review*, *69*(5), 1114–1132. https://doi.org/10.1177/0019793916660508

Stamm, B. H. (2010) *The Concise ProQOL Manual* (2nd ed.). Pocatello, ID: ProQOL.org.

Stelitano, L., Doan, S., Woo, A., Diliberti, M. K., Kaufman, J. H., & Henry, D. (n.d.). *The digital divide and COVID-19: Teachers' perceptions of inequities in students' internet access and participation in remote learning*. RAND Corporation. Retrieved February 3, 2024, from https://www.rand.org.

Yancy, C. W. (2020). COVID-19 and African Americans. *JAMA*, *323*(19), 1891–1892.

4

Addressing Compassion Fatigue in Yourself

In Chapter 3, I shared the findings of two studies that shed some interesting light on teachers' experiences with compassion fatigue. In this chapter we will explore strategies to mitigate compassion fatigue and self-care strategies you could utilize to take care of yourself while teaching some of which are suggestions from fellow teachers.

Recall that research illuminates the precarious predicament we are in as a school system. Our students clearly are struggling, but as result of their struggle teachers are too. The descriptions of burnout and secondary trauma clearly belay just how much stress teachers are under. The themes capture just how difficult it is for teachers to remain compassionate in the face of such trauma. And let's be honest, those experiences are daunting. So much so that they cannot be left unaddressed. Compassion fatigue unaddressed can cause detrimental effects on a teacher's mental, physical, and emotional health (Secondary Traumatic Stress, n.d.). Now understandably, healing compassion fatigue is a subjective journey given its impact on an individual, but I believe, and research and experts have shown, that there are things that can be done systemically to address it. But before we review what researchers and experts have to say, let's hear directly from teachers experiencing compassion. What is it they say will help them to feel more supported, less burned out, less stressed?

What Fellow Teachers Say Would Help Them Thrive

When I asked several groups of educators (teachers, administrators, and counselors) what support would help them thrive so that I could better understand the type of support needed to combat teacher compassion fatigue, they had a lot to say. For example, when asked what supports teachers needed or wished they had but may or may not be currently receiving, *Alex, Middle School Teacher*, recommended that school site administration intentionally attend to the social-emotional needs of staff on a continuous and consistent basis (Ollison, 2019). *Abby, Middle School Teacher,* would like annual mandatory educator self-care talks (Ollison, 2019). Teachers also expressed that teacher care should be provided in addition to student care whenever there are traumatic events at school – especially for student suicides (Ollison, 2019). Figure 4.1 captures the support teachers expressed a desire to have.

As you read the description of each of the requested supports below try to reflect on whether you agree or disagree with their recommendations. Then think about how you might personally implement the suggested supports. Several of the recommendations were geared toward issues that emerged during the pandemic. All of the suggestions highlight areas that relate to support systems, practices, and policy areas of need.

Requested Supports
Supportive Administration
- It is important for administrators to show their appreciation for, support, and understanding of the daily challenges teachers face. This can be done by acknowledging the difficulty of the work, providing teacher-informed support

Addressing Compassion Fatigue in Yourself ◆ 87

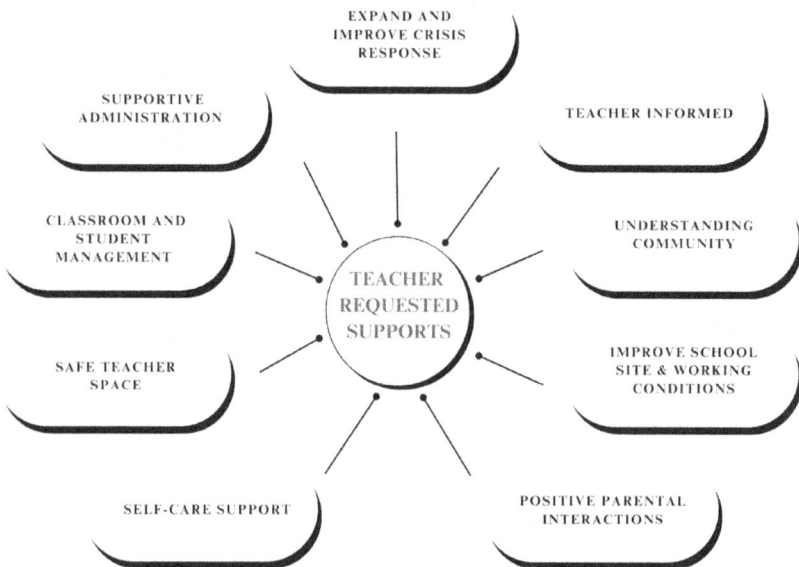

FIGURE 4.1 Teacher-Requested Support (Ollison, 2019)

and practices, and intentionally checking in with staff who appear to be struggling.

Teacher-Informed Support

♦ Emphasize the importance of and need for teacher support. Support should be defined by teachers themselves and not by others for teachers and should include opportunities for peer support in addition to administrative support.

Classroom Management and Student Support

♦ Provide more training in classroom management to ensure teachers can show compassion and empathy with all their students – not resentment. The pandemic exacerbated behavior issues among students, parents, and in some cases collegial misconduct (McMahon et al., 2022). Refresh training content to include recommendations for addressing the new normal of poor student behavior.

Cultivate Safe Teacher Space
- Create safe spaces for teacher voices to be heard. School districts and schoool sites can emotionally support teachers by providing a space for them to share their experiences with other staff, especially administrators. The support could be just to listen or to help. Ensure that the emotional support provided is informed by expressed needs of teachers. That is, ask teachers directly what they need in that space.

Develop an Understanding of the School Community
- Ensure staff know the characteristics and nuances of the community of students they serve. Intentionally address the school's climate with explicit conversations about the climate with all staff in staff meetings.

Improve School Site Working Conditions for Teachers and Students
- Adjust class-size ratios, provide more classified staff support in special education classrooms, and enforce school rules consistently and fairly. Repair things that are broken and supply students with resources they will need to be successful. Eliminate disparities in treatment and resources between low- and high-poverty schools.

Self-Care Support
- Provide mandatory professional development on educator self-care and compassion fatigue, including encouragement to participate in the trainings without judgment.

Positive Parental Interaction
- Develop training for teachers to actively engage with parents in a positive way. Create ways for parents to show they value teachers too and ensure parents understand the impact that appreciating teachers can have on the classroom environment.

Expand and Improve Crisis Response
- ♦ Include teachers as recipients of support in addition to students whenever traumatic events occur. Increase the number of crisis trainings that occur so teachers can be better equipped to deal with them when they occur.

Hire More Support Staff
- ♦ During the pandemic hiring of essential staff was difficult. This led to administrators and teachers taking on more work just to manage the day-to-day demand. Support requests for more aides in the classroom to help with behavioral issues and workload management. A call for additional support staff such as Multitiered System of Support (MTSS) coordinators, campus monitors, and social workers to help manage increased student needs was also expressed.

Mental Health Resources for Staff
- ♦ While there was a recognition of more trauma and mental health support needed for students the adults also requested this support. Specifically, there were calls for grief counseling, mental health support for staff, and recognition of the emotional labor teachers are performing. And while we are a few years out of the COVID-19 pandemic these calls are still relevant today (Mathews & Hart Research Associates, 2022).

Financial, Professional, and Moral Support
- ♦ These areas are a common trope among educators with regard to requested areas of increased support (Dixon et al., 2019; Podolsky et al., 2016). There is still a need for better compensation, acknowledgment of the hard work being done, and moral support from district leaders and the educational community at large. The pandemic increased people's desire to have the following: increased advocacy for better pay for instructional aides, financial incentives for all staff, and professional development focusing on coping strategies and compassion fatigue.

Tool 4.1 – What do you Search, Evaluate, and Adapt (S.E.A.)?

Overview: A tool designed to help you find and adapt or create a strategy for self-care based on the ***teacher-requested supports*** recommended by your teacher peers (See Figure 4.1).

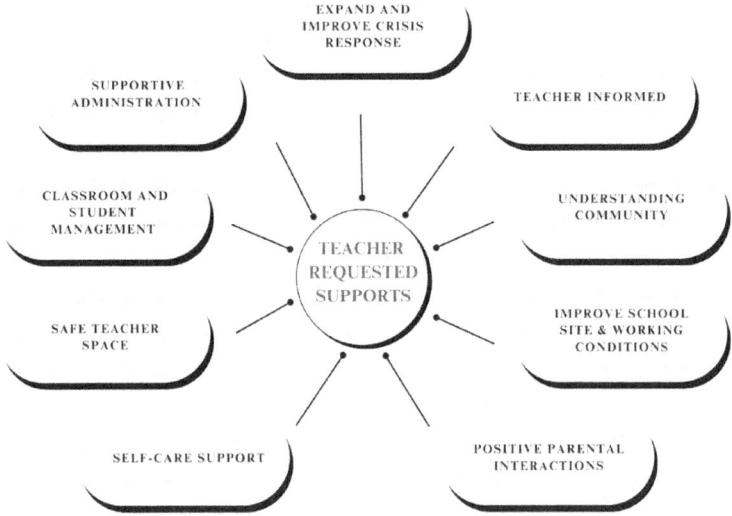

Directions: In addition to the suggestions shared in this section, many examples of these types of support exist online. Go exploring and find a strategy that you think would be interesting or fun to use (or adapt for use) for self-care. Answer the questions as you do. **Search Term Suggestions:** Search for the terms listed in *Figure 4.1*.

Question Prompts	*Response Notes*
1. Describe the activity and provide a website.	
2. Explain how you might adapt it to fit your personal lifestyle and your teaching lifestyle.	
3. Explain how you think it will help you practice self-care and combat compassion fatigue.	
4. Explain how you think it will help you to improve your professional quality of life.	
5. Commit to trying your newly adapted activity at least one time a week for the next three weeks.	

Support for Better Work-Life Boundaries
- The demands of the pandemic made it difficult for some to maintain a clear boundary between work and home. While most teachers always take work home to plan or to grade, teachers are seeking more defined boundaries to prevent work from intruding into their personal lives. It would be helpful if the school system recognized and supported this goal with shifts in workload and demands on time before-and-after school, and on weekends.

 Pause and Reflect: Which of the recommendations would you most like to see enacted at your school site or school district? Why? What would you most like to try personally?

What Research Says Would Help to Heal Compassion Fatigue

Research shows that most people who work with traumatized people are empathetic and will likely experience compassion fatigue at some point in their career (Mathieu, 2011; Treating Compassion Fatigue, 2002). The good news is that compassion fatigue is manageable. Awareness of its presence is half the battle (Figley, 1995; Monk, 2023). The other half includes taking definitive steps to address its impact and manifestation in one's life. Here are just a few research-recommended healing approaches that will help with your healing process. Monk (2023) suggests that to heal and prevent compassion fatigue, professionals can focus on five key strategies:

Mind, Body, Heart, and Spirit Replenishment
- Prioritize daily practices that nourish mental, physical, emotional, and spiritual health. As the tools of their trade, professionals' energy, vitality, and attitude contribute to their effectiveness. Consistent self-care is essential to prevent burnout and sustain fulfillment over time.

Access and Nurture Support
- Seek emotional support, peer support, and supervision to mitigate the risk of compassion fatigue. Social support

is a crucial predictor of professionals' well-being, emphasizing the importance of caring for one another and avoiding isolation.

Stay Connected to Meaning
- Maintain a connection to the hope, joy, purpose, and meaning within the profession. Research shows that this connection reduces the risk of burnout and compassion fatigue. Reflect on what brings joy and fulfillment as a helper.

Engage in Reflective Practice
- Practice mindfulness, reflective journaling, and self-awareness to prevent compassion fatigue. By staying present and attuned to their own needs, professionals can cultivate resilience and renewal.

Be Kind to Yourself
- Practice self-compassion and treat oneself with the same care and concern shown to others. Recognize the importance of self-kindness in sustaining the capacity for compassion and preventing burnout.

By implementing these strategies, Monk (2023) argues that professionals can cultivate resilience, maintain well-being, and sustain their capacity for compassion while preventing the onset of compassion fatigue. In addition, the Center for Victims of Torture (CVT) (2021) recommends that self-care practices can help prevent the development of compassion fatigue. These practices can help educators to manage stress, enhance their well-being, and prevent the onset of compassion fatigue and thus support their ability to provide compassionate-centered education to students who need it most. What's more, by focusing on building one's strengths and carrying out self-care activities it can help contribute to behavioral, cognitive, physical, spiritual, and emotional resilience (CVT, 2021). Table 4.1 contains a summary of specific practices mentioned to build resiliency that will be helpful for teachers.

TABLE 4.1 Self-Care Practices to Boost Resiliency

Develop Positive Work Habits

- Core Components of Resilience: Focus on adequate sleep, good nutrition, regular physical activity, and active relaxation techniques such as yoga, meditation, and relaxation exercises.
- Team Cohesiveness: Engage with colleagues to celebrate successes and mourn sorrows collectively.
- Workload Management: Reduce workload intensity and repetitiveness and integrate variety into work where possible.
- Mentorship: Seek guidance from a mentor, supervisor, or experienced colleague to enhance the work environment and promote work-life balance.
- Breaks from Work: Take time away from work when possible and find things to look forward to. Relationships and Social Support: Nurture positive personal and professional relationships and develop social support networks.
- Professional Support and Learning: Seek professional support and be open to learning new skills for personal and professional well-being.

Focus on Your Physical and Spiritual Well-being

- Sleep and Hydration: Ensure adequate rest and stay hydrated.
- Healthy Diet: Maintain a balanced and healthy diet.
- Nature: Spend time in nature regularly.
- Spiritual Practices: Practice spiritual beliefs or seek support from faith leaders.
- Purpose and Meaning: Find meaning or purpose in daily activities and remind yourself of the significance of your work.
- Social Connections: Make time to learn about and connect with colleagues.
- Rituals and Boundaries: Create individual ceremonies or rituals to help separate work from personal life, such as changing clothes after work or having a specific routine to mark the transition from work to home.
- Self-compassion: Practice self-compassion and kindness toward oneself.

Focus on The Positive

- Self-reflection and Rest: Take time to be alone for reflection, grounding, and rest.
- Positive Thinking: Challenge negative internal dialogue and focus on adopting a more positive outlook.
- Self-awareness: Build self-awareness through mindfulness and reflection practices.

Source: CVT. (2021). Compassion fatigue. In *The Center for Victims of Torture (CVT)*. Visit https://proqol.org/compassion-fatigue for more information.

> ***Pause and Reflect:*** *Of the recommendations for healing compassion fatigue what would you most like to try personally? Why?*

Compassion Fatigue Hall Pass Tool

Now that you have spent some time reflecting, here is a practical tool you can use to support your own compassion fatigue healing journey. I recommend you spend at least 45 minutes working through this tool. You're worth it! The **Compassion Fatigue Hall Pass** is a resource designed for teachers to proactively address and manage the impacts of compassion fatigue. This practical guide offers a structured and customizable framework for personal or professional application. As a self-care instrument, it enhances the professional quality of life for teachers and others in emotionally demanding roles. It uses a methodical approach to aid teachers to identify, acknowledge, and address personal signs and symptoms of compassion fatigue. It is an essential asset for fostering self-awareness, promoting diligent self-care practices, and ensuring sustainability in the teaching profession.

Tool 4.2 – My Compassion Fatigue Hall Pass

Description: A tool to help you address your own experience with compassion fatigue as an act of self-care to have an improved professional quality of life.

- P. Personal
- A. Acknowledgment
- S. Signs and Symptoms
- S. Strategies, Skills, and Tools

P. Personal

Goal: To Become Aware of What Is Happening to You in Your Workspace

Write a response to the following question: How are your experiences with trauma in the school setting similar or different from educators experiencing compassion fatigue? Explain.

A. Acknowledgment

Goal: To Descriptively Share Specific Examples of Your Experiences

Fill in the blank: As I reflect on my own experiences, I have worked with students who have experienced trauma such as …

S. Signs and Symptoms

Goal: To Become Aware of Ways in Which the Trauma Is Affecting You

Fill in the blank: These experiences affect me in the following ways (Describe ways it affected you or your ability to do the work) …

S. Strategies, Skills, and Tools

Goal: To Make a Plan of Strategies, Skills, and Tools You Can Use to Help Yourself Heal

Review the list of suggested strategies, skills, and tools. **Select two** that you will commit to using when you find yourself in need. Explain when you will use each of the tools selected.

- Feel your feelings.
- Share your feelings.
- Journaling.
- Co-listening practice.
- Seek mental health support.
- Stay connected with the community.
- Do one thing for self-care every day or at least weekly (e.g., Sundays).
- Subscribe to a meditation app like headspace or calm. Then use it once a week at least.
- Set weekly or daily intentions (example here: https://youtu.be/LAFhiiDfii0).
- Meditate.
- Practice mindfulness – attention paid to the present moment.
- 5-4-3-2-1 Method (learn more here: https://youtu.be/30VMIEmA114).
- Place a symbol, trinket, picture, or object in your classroom or office to use a visual reminder to breathe.
- Perform body scans (example here: https://youtu.be/zNfv4UDBk6w).
- Breathe (use various meditations).
- Incorporate check-in/check-out processes for meetings and classes.
- Dance.
- Exercise.

Reflect on your selected strategy, skill, or tool.
What did you select for the first tool? Why did you select it? When will you use it? How will you use it?

What did you select for the second tool? Why did you select it? When will you use it? How will you use it?

Healing Compassion Fatigue with Systemic Action

Educator-Focused Multitiered System of Support (EMTSS)

I believe an EMTSS aimed at promoting a healthy and robust teacher workforce at all levels, PreK-12, should be developed to support educator compassion fatigue. The goal is to ensure that we support the professional quality of educators in ways that help them to have and show awareness of compassion fatigue and educator self-care, establish self-care goals, and make progress toward meeting their own adult social-emotional needs in order to maintain a healthy school and classroom environments.

The three tiers should address supports aimed at **all teachers** who are entering or already a part of the teaching profession, **some teachers** who work specifically at urban school sites with large populations of historically marginalized students, and **few teachers** who work at schools in extreme crisis such as from natural disasters, school shootings, and suicide clusters (OCDE, n.d.). These tiers offer recommendations for different levels of support, ranging from universal strategies applicable to all staff to more targeted interventions for those experiencing significant challenges. Although the recommendations are separated by tiers, they can be enacted as needed in any order.

The EMTSS should contain recommended strategies that promote teacher retention through the healing of compassion fatigue. The recommendations illuminate components that should be included within EMTSS delineated by tier and address actions state- and local-level policymakers can take. These recommendations cast a broad net over the education landscape because they target areas that shift how teachers are prepared, expected to perform, and supported. The recommendations are intentionally modeled after California's marquee component of the system of support aimed at improving school climate and conditions for student learning – the Multitiered System of Support (MTSS). MTSS is "a method of organization" (CDE, 2017) used to align existing resources and initiatives to "promote the building of a stronger student academic and behavioral support system at the local level" (California Department of Education & State Board of Education, 2023, p. 106). See Figure 4.2.

I originally published these in 2019, and since that time compassion fatigue, secondary trauma, and burnout have made their way more into the mainstream, but comprehensive plans to

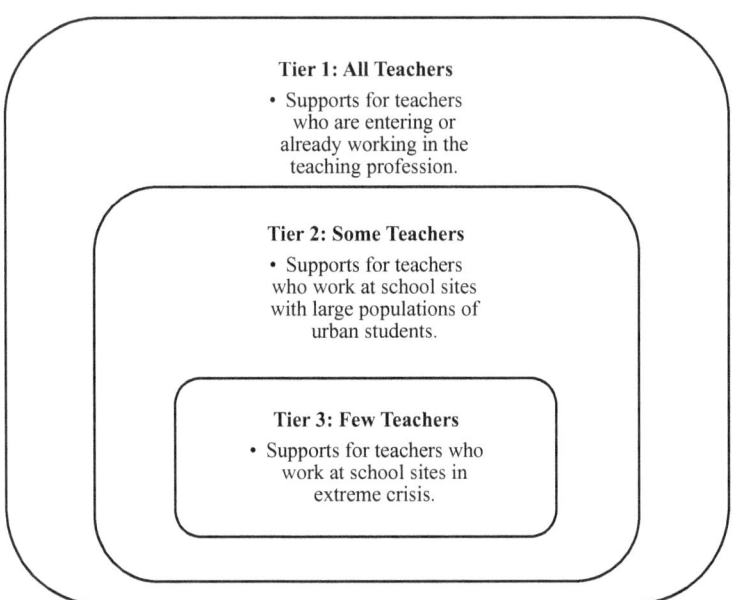

FIGURE 4.2 Educator-Focused Multitiered System of Support (EMTSS) (Ollison, 2019)

teacher compassion fatigue, specifically, at the personal, school site, school district, county, and state levels are still warranted. I now share a few of the recommendations here. They are ones that I feel are most relevant to this discussion about supporting teachers to combat compassion fatigue. Please note that even though the recommendations written are separated by state and local levels all are relevant to teachers as teachers can either enact them personally or insist on collective action their school site, district, and with state level actors. If you are interested in the original version, please look them up in my dissertation "Improving Teacher Retention by Addressing Teachers Compassion Fatigue" (Ollison, 2019).

Tier I Recommendations: All Teachers

- **State Level**
  - Update standards for the teaching profession to include recognition of compassion fatigue as an occupational hazard for educators, especially those who work with traumatized students (Figley, 1995).
  - Develop mandatory professional development training focused on compassion fatigue, educator self-care strategies, adult social-emotional learning (SEL) strategies, and mental health first aid (MHFA) crisis response that support the health and well-being of students and staff (National Council for Mental Wellbeing, 2023). All PreK-12 educators (certificated and classified) should take this training.
  - Expand teaching performance expectations to include the recognition of compassion fatigue. For example, teachers should be supported to understand and recognize indicators that students might be experiencing trauma or crisis so that they can help students get the necessary support they need.
  - A course on compassion fatigue and secondary trauma should be included in preliminary multiple-subject and single-subject program standards. The course should introduce compassion fatigue and how it is measured,

such as through the Professional Quality of Life Scale (Stamm, 2010). In addition, the course should explain symptoms for individuals and organizations, factors that influence susceptibility, mitigation strategies, and self-care strategies (Figley, 1995). Similar updates should also occur in Administrative Credential Programs.

- Credential program design and curriculum must be updated to ensure teachers are adequately prepared to meet the needs of urban students. Updates should address trauma in urban students, as well as its effects on their social, academic, and behavioral performance. In addition, they should address the educators who support them. Administrative credential programs need the same updates.

- Credential programs (teacher and administrator) should include learning about unconscious bias. It should assist teachers in understanding how their own hidden biases may be impacting their behavior and perceptions of urban students, especially when they are experiencing burnout and secondary trauma.

♦ *Local Level*

- Increase the quality, availability, and access to stellar family engagement resources. Resources should recognize the dual nature of the parent-teacher relationship. Resources should also help educators and parents communicate effectively.

- Engage in practices to strengthen trust, partnership, and relationships between administrators and their staff, such as the California Labor Management Initiative (CA LMI). See CA LMI at https://cdefoundation.org/cde_programs/clmi/.

- In all schools, conditions and climate should be improved. Engage teachers in conversations about school climate as a way to improve. Conduct annual climate surveys and review the results using the data, meaning, and use cycle recommended by the California State Board of Education School Conditions and Climate work group (California Department of Education [CDE], 2017). The data, meaning, and use cycle are described on page 28 of the School Climate and Conditions Workgroup Recommendations Report at https://www.cde.ca.gov/be/pn/im/documents/memo-ocd-oct17item01a1.pdf.

Tier 2 Recommendations: Some Teachers

- *State Level*

  - Increase budget allocations to urban school sites to ensure adequate financial resources. Students should have access to the same technology, curriculum, and programs as low-poverty schools.

  - Work with teacher union leadership to ensure urban schools have access to highly qualified and experienced teachers.

- *Local Level*

  - Administrators should acknowledge the difficulty of teaching, provide teacher-informed support and practices, and intentionally and regularly check-in with staff who appear to be struggling in order to demonstrate that they care, appreciate, and understand (Pennington, 2017).

  - Improve the effectiveness of staff meetings by establishing check-in and check-out procedures (Kofman, 2018).

  - Provide adult SEL support to school site staff (certified and classified) by adopting practices that enable educators to "effectively apply knowledge, attitudes, and skills to understand and manage emotions, set and achieve positive goals, feel empathy for others, form relationships, and make responsible decisions" (CDE, 2017, p. 2).

- Use the restorative justice practice of dialogue circles to address the self-care, processing, and support needs of school site staff (certified and classified) after trauma, such as suicides or particularly distressing interactions with students (Darling-Hammond & Darling-Hammond, 2024).

Tier 3 Recommendations: Few Teachers

- **State Level**
  - Ensure effective response to mental health needs of students, staff, and families post natural disasters by:
    - Offering mental health services to those affected by crises such as wildfires, school shootings, and suicide clusters.
  - Facilitating statewide efforts to address trauma and mental health needs, including:
  - Establishing a statewide crisis response and recovery team and train them using PREPaRE (About PREPaRE, n.d.). For more information, visit https://www.nasponline.org/professional-development/prepare-training-curriculum/about-prepare.
  - Providing professional development for trauma and Mental Health First Aid (MHFA).
  - Creating a regularly vetted and updated list of mental health service providers for support.
  - Developing a comprehensive "high-quality school emergency operations plan" encompassing Prevention, Protection, Mitigation, Response, and Recovery (REMS TA Center, n.d.). It should also include information regarding addressing mental health emergencies. Visit *Guides For Developing Emergency Operations Plans* on the Readiness and Emergency Management for Schools Technical Assistance Center website at https://rems.ed.gov/EOPGuides for more information.

Pause and Reflect: *Describe your reaction to EMTSS.*

Engaging in Your Own Educator-Focused Multitiered System of Support (EMTSS) Tool

The **Engaging in Your Own Educator-Focused Multitiered System of Support (EMTSS)** tool guides educators on how to implement an Educator-Focused Multitiered System of Support (EMTSS). It emphasizes providing support at multiple levels to address educators' varying needs. This is done by including locally designed strategies to mitigate compassion fatigue, enhance professional development, and improve overall teacher retention. This tool will help you consider how to apply EMTSS in your own institutions, using the provided research-based tiers of recommendations for action. By the time you are finished you will have the beginning of a plan to develop and implement support systems that are responsive to teachers' needs, enhancing their well-being and effectiveness. If you prefer, you can also use it to consider how to apply EMTSS to yourself. In that case, each tier level refers to times when you might need increasingly more intensive support.

Toll 4.3 – Engaging in Your Own EMTSS Process

Directions: Consider the recommendations presented in Chapter 4. Respond to the questions below. Then Develop a clear action plan outlining how the EMTSS will be implemented, including timelines, responsible parties, and specific interventions at each tier. Make sure to consider how your EMTSS will be integrated with existing policies and practices within the school or school district to support coherence and sustainability. If you prefer, you can also use it to consider how to apply EMTSS to yourself. In that case, each tier level refers to times when you might need increasingly more intensive support.

Which of the Recommendations for Tier 1: All Teachers resonate most with you? List all that apply. Why?

> *Universal supports for teachers who are entering or already working in the profession.*

Which of the Recommendations for Tier 2: Some Teachers resonate most with you? List all that apply. Why?

> *Supports for teachers who work at school sites with large populations of historically marginalized students.*

Which of the Recommendations for Tier 3: Few Teachers resonate most with you? List all that apply. Why?

> *Supports for teachers who work at school sites in extreme crisis.*

Tier Description	Action Steps - School/ District or Personal Focus	Responsible Party	Timeline
Tier 1: All Teachers	(What resources do you want to do for all educators?)		
Tier 2: Some Teachers	(What resources do you want to do for some educators?)		
Tier 3: Few Teachers	(What resources do you want to do for a few educators?)		

Over the last few chapters, it has been shown that compassion fatigue is a real concern for teachers. This chapter discussed how to intentionally deal with compassion fatigue personally and professionally. Please know that your journey to healing can be supported regardless of where you are on it. In my heart, I know that teachers know what they need, and we need to listen to them and design support based on that listening. The recommendations in this chapter will help you get started. Now it is up to you to do your part to help mitigate the effects of compassion fatigue.

 Connect the Thoughts

1. What surprising or significant knowledge did you gain from this chapter?
2. What connections do you see to yourself? your school site? school district?
3. How might you help strengthen school site working conditions and climate so that teachers will be supported to thrive socially, emotionally, and professionally?
4. Which of the tools most resonate with you? Why?
5. How might you use this information to improve your professional quality of life?

References

About PREPaRE. (n.d.). National Association of School Psychologists (NASP). Retrieved June 17, 2024, from https://www.nasponline.org/professional-development/prepare-training-curriculum/about-prepare

California Department of Education [CDE]. (2017). School conditions and climate work group recommendation framework. *State Board of Education*. Retrieved June 17, 2024, from https://www.cde.ca.gov/be/pn/im/documents/memo-ocd-oct17item01a1.pdf

California Department of Education & State Board of Education. (2023). *California ESSA Consolidated State Plan*. Retrieved September 8, 2024, from https://oese.ed.gov/files/2023/12/ca-state-plan-2023.pdf

CVT. (2021). Compassion fatigue. *The Center for Victims of Torture (CVT)*. Retrieved February 15, 2024, from https://proqol.org/compassion-fatigue

Darling-Hammond, L., & Darling-Hammond, S. (2024). *Brown at 70: Progress, pushback, and policies that matter*. Spencer Foundation, Learning Policy Institute, California Association of African-American Superintendents and Administrators. Retrieved September 8, 2024, from https://www.spencer.org/learning/brown-at-70-progress-pushback-and-policies-that-matter

Dixon, D., Griffin, A., & Teoh, M. (2019). If you listen, we will stay: why teachers of color leave and how to disrupt teacher turnover. *The Education Trust*. Retrieved June 17, 2024, from https://files.eric.ed.gov/fulltext/ED603193.pdf

Figley, C. R. (1995). Compassion fatigue as secondary traumatic stress disorder: An overview. In C. R. Figley (ed.), *Compassion fatigue: Coping with secondary traumatic stress disorder in those who treat the traumatized* (Psychosocial Stress Series) (Kindle Edition) (Vol. 1, pp. 1–18). New York: Taylor and Francis.

Kofman, F. (2018, March 23). *Check in, check out: a tool for "Real" conversations – The Systems Thinker*. The Systems Thinker. Retrieved June 17, 2024, from https://thesystemsthinker.com/check-in-check-out-a-tool-for-real-conversations/

Mathews, K., Ph. D., & Hart Research Associates. (2022). *Voices from the classroom: Developing a strategy for teacher retention and recruitment:*

Key findings from a survey of TK-12 teachers in California and in-depth interviews with aspiring and former teachers in California. Retrieved February 3, 2024, from, https://transformschools.ucla.edu/research/voices-from-the-classroom/

Mathieu, F. (2011). *The compassion fatigue workbook: Creative tools for transforming compassion fatigue and vicarious traumatization.* Retrieved June 17, 2024, from https://openlibrary.org/books/OL25025170M/The_compassion_fatigue_workbook

McMahon, S. D., Anderman, E. M., Astor, R. A., Espelage, D. L., Martinez, A., Reddy, L. A., & Worrell, F. C. (2022). *Violence against educators and school personnel: Crisis during COVID: Technical report.* American Psychological Association. Retrieved July 23, 2023, from https://www.apa.org/education-career/k12/violence-educators-technical-report.pdf

Monk, L. (2023, August 10). 5 pathways for healing compassion fatigue. *Crisis & Trauma Resource Institute.* Retrieved June 17, 2024, from https://ctrinstitute.com/blog/5-pathways-healing-compassion-fatigue/

National Council for Mental Wellbeing. (2023, September 18). *Mental health first aid.* Retrieved June 17, 2024, from https://www.thenationalcouncil.org/our-work/mental-health-first-aid/

Ollison, J. (2019). *Improving teacher retention by addressing teachers' compassion fatigue.* Scholarly Commons. Retrieved February 3, 2024, from https://scholarlycommons.pacific.edu/uop_etds/3602/

Pennington, R. (2017, August 15). The power of appreciation to transform your culture . . . and your business. *HuffPost.* Retrieved June 17, 2024, from https://www.huffpost.com/entry/the-power-of-appreciation-to-transform-your-culture_b_59908a6ae4b063e2ae058098

Podolsky, A., Kini, T., Bishop, J. B., & Darling-Hammond, L. (2016). *Solving the teacher shortage: How to attract and retain excellent educators.* Palo Alto, CA: Learning Policy Institute. Retrieved June 17, 2024, from https://doi.org/10.54300/262.960

Stamm, B. H. (2010). *The Concise ProQOL Manual* (2nd ed.). Pocatello, ID: ProQOL.org.

Treating compassion fatigue. (2002). In C. Figley (Ed.), *Routledge eBooks* (1st ed.). Routledge. Retrieved June 17, 2024, from https://doi.org/10.4324/9780203890318

5

Sowing Seeds of Resilience

I could summarize the entire book for you here in this chapter, but I want to do something other than that. You've seen me talking about compassion fatigue and its impact on teachers in urban schools more than enough. In Chapter 1, I discussed the nature of urban schools and how their design is linked to harmful public policy decisions like the 1938 Federal Housing Act. You can refer to Chapter 1 if you need a refresher. In Chapter 2, I delved more deeply into compassion fatigue, its symptoms, and who will most likely experience it. In Chapter 3, I shared research exploring the impacts of compassion fatigue on teachers before and during the pandemic. In Chapter 4, strategies to combat compassion fatigue coupled with several practical tools that could be utilized to help you do it were offered. In this chapter, I will further illuminate the seeds of resilience sown throughout the book. As you work to address compassion fatigue personally and professionally, these seeds of information will be helpful in your journey.

Seed 1 – Urban Students Deserve Happy, Healthy, Thriving Teachers Who Will See Their Humanity

Every urban student deserves an education that will equip them with the knowledge and skills necessary to live a successful life. This hinges on having healthy, happy, quality teachers who see their humanity and endeavor to teach in ways that support their students' dreams. Unfortunately, that is not exactly what happens on a daily basis.

Urban students face systemic social and academic inequities that hinder their educational attainment. Segregation by race and income leads to the clustering of low-income Black and Hispanic families in disadvantaged communities, resulting in disparities in school services, resources, and quality of teachers. The inequities urban students face are by design. The United States government-sanctioned structural racism, such as the Federal Housing Act of 1938, laid the foundation for years of economic and environmental abuses and harms that are still occurring today. Harms that include food deserts, environmental pollutants, inadequate access to parks and services, and, yes, under-resourced and understaffed schools.

Urban areas, particularly those with concentrated poverty, face high levels of community violence. This violence disproportionately affects children, leading to traumatic experiences and potential student mental health challenges such as post-traumatic stress disorder (PTSD), which can manifest in various academic and behavioral problems in school settings. My research shows that a statistically significant positive relationship between a school's socioeconomic status and compassion fatigue (burnout and secondary trauma) exists. That is, as the socioeconomically disadvantaged status of the school increases, so do teacher burnout and secondary trauma scores.

This is why it is imperative that teachers are given proper training and support to ensure they can do right by urban students. All teachers of urban students should understand trauma-informed practices. They should also be trained in mental health first aid, focusing on youth. For example, the organization

Mental Health FIRST AID from the National Council for Mental Wellbeing offers training with content that covers familiar youth mental health concerns, stigma reduction, how to recognize mental health and substance abuse signs, and it provides a five-step action plan to assist youth in crisis, including those at risk of suicide (*Youth – Mental Health First Aid*, 2023). This type of training and content should be baked into every teacher preparation program and professional development plan. It should be mandatory, like cardiopulmonary resuscitation (CPR) first aid training. It is essential to improving teachers' professional quality of life and teaching skill set. And it might help teachers to save a student's life, too.

> **Pause and Reflect:** *Would you like to be trained in youth-focused mental health first aid? Why or why not?*
>
> **Act:** *Visit Mental Health First Aid from The National Council for Mental Wellbeing at https://www.mentalhealthfirstaid.org/population-focused-modules/youth/*

Seed 2 – Addressing Compassion Fatigue Improves Teachers Efficacy

"Employees who work with trauma victims, especially traumatized children, may be leaving their jobs because they too have become traumatized and, as a result, suffer from symptoms that affect their ability to function" (Figley, 2002, p. 42). That is, when people suffer from compassion fatigue, their ability to do their jobs, including engaging in healthy relationships, is hampered.

Stress is pernicious. The two most recognized acute stress responses to trauma are fight or flight (Figley, 2002). Instinctually, our brains are wired to survive, which fighting or fleeing helps us do (Figley, 2002). Figley (2002) asserts that when helping professionals use empathy in their practice, they open themselves up to receive the traumatic information and stress their client shares, known as transference. However, given that the "intimate relationship between helpers and victims is a two-way affair" (p. 20), it is possible that the helper also transfers their traumatic issues and stress to the client, known as countertransference. Unfortunately, "when helpers' survival strategies are insufficient to resolve victim stresses, helpers become secondarily stressed by carrying both maladaptive [inadequate] victim survival strategies with which they identify and their own maladaptive complementary survival strategies, which become insufficient" (p. 25). In other words, they compound each other's trauma (p. 20).

It is possible that within the four walls of the classroom, students and teachers are compounding each other's trauma (Figley, 2002; Wolpow et al., 2009). Teachers and students may be reacting to and triggering one another while both in a state of heightened anxiety. The prolonged nature of this could cause burnout symptoms such as irritability, anxiousness, aggression, callousness, pessimism, and diminished work performance. It can also cause secondary traumatic stress symptoms like over-involvement or avoidance behaviors like numbness or withdrawal from the relationship (Figley, 2002). The typical stress survival strategy of flight is not an option within the classroom, and teachers, unaware that they are suffering from compassion fatigue, may have no recourse but to fight or freeze. The prolonged nature can also lead to toxic stress, which can lead to increased health risks and diminished cognitive function in children (Harris, 2018).

Unfortunately, teachers' responses in these hyper-aroused states may lead to extreme negative repercussions for urban students, including excessive punitive punishments like suspension and expulsions (Wood et al., 2018). For example, The National Center for Education Statistics [NCES] (2022) shows in the latest data they have for suspension that African American students are **three times more** likely to be suspended or expelled when compared to White students. And **four times more** likely to be suspended more than once. They are also approximately **two times more likely** to be referred to law enforcement when expelled. See Table 5.1 for more details.

TABLE 5.1 Summary of Selected Disciplinary Actions in United States Public Elementary and Secondary Schools, by Race/Ethnicity: 2017–2018

Ethnicity of Students	Total out of School Suspension	More than One Suspension	Total Expulsion	Expelled Referral to Law Enforcement	Total Student Population by Race	Total of Student Population Overall
White	604,202	208,888	26,057	61,135	23,977,160	47%
%	2.52%	0.87%	0.11%	0.25%		
Black	603550	273947	25457	41535	7675380	15%
%	7.86%	3.57%	0.33%	0.54%		
Hispanic	369,949	126,513	15,523	12656	13,673,000	27%
%	2.71%	0.93%	0.11%	0.09%		

National Center for Education Statistics [NCES] (2022).

Recall that the research presented in Chapter 3 showed statistical analyses that revealed that compassion fatigue in teachers correlates strongly with the school's racial demographics. Schools with higher percentages of White students see increased compassion satisfaction and decreased burnout and secondary traumatic stress among teachers. Conversely, higher percentages of African American students correlate with lower compassion satisfaction and higher burnout and secondary traumatic stress. This suggests that teachers may harbor unconscious biases, influencing their stress levels and student interactions. Bias (an opinion), is often hidden or unconscious (Banaji & Greenwald, 2016). These biases align with societal patterns, as evidenced by implicit association test (IAT) results showing a prevalent automatic White preference among all Americans (Banaji & Greenwald, 2016; Xu et al., 2018).

Considering this with the correlation tests that revealed statistically significant relationships between compassion fatigue and the school's racial demographics and socioeconomic status, it can be quite disconcerting. Especially since in hyper-aroused states, one is instinctively attuned to self-protecting, often causing anxiety and physical and emotional exhaustion (Figley,

2002). In other words, teachers' minds are elsewhere, which is critical to note because talking or thinking about race-related bias issues like this correlation can evoke emotional responses like anger, shame, guilt, and despair (Tatum, 1992). These types of situations do not leave much room for clear thinking, political correctness, bias-free behavior, or grace.

This is why addressing teacher's compassion fatigue is so important. It sets the stage for teachers to engage effectively with students and create learning environments that recognize and meet students' and teachers' social, emotional, and human needs.

 Pause and Reflect: *How might addressing Compassion Fatigue support your practice?*

☐ **Act:** *Visit Project Implicit and Take an Implicit Association Test (IAT) to uncover any unconscious attitudes or beliefs you may have at https://implicit.harvard.edu/implicit/takeatest.html*

Seed 3 – Teachers and Administrators Are on the Same Team

Pre-pandemic, my research showed that sometimes the trauma teachers experience is school conditions and climate-based and related to interactions with parents or school site administration. The implication that school administrators do not always understand the teacher's everyday classroom experience and that parents are not supposed to be the enemy but sometimes feel that way was a common thread through all interviews. Teachers also had concerns about how actions taken by school environment actors, including parents, students, other teachers, and administrators, affected their ability to create safe and academically challenging environments. It also impacted the teacher's morale.

When compassion fatigue reaches the organization level, symptoms may include the "Inability for teams to work well together, strong reluctance toward change, [and an] inability of staff to believe improvement is possible" (Ollison, 2019, p. 49).

But the pandemic leveled the playing field. Post-pandemic teachers could better see that teachers and administrators were "in it" together. Teachers could see that their administrators were working to ensure that teachers had what they needed to teach and thrive to the best of their ability. Showing just how important a school's climate and working conditions are to the relationships between teachers and administrators.

Strong staff and student relationships are vital to a positive school climate and working conditions (California Department of Education [CDE], 2017). The character and quality of the school (Collie et al., 2012, p. 1191) and the values, expectations, interpersonal relationships, critical resources, supports, and practices that foster or inhibit a welcoming, inclusive, and academically challenging environment are also crucial (California Department of Education [CDE], 2017). Rubinstein and McCarthy (2016) have proven that when positive collaborative relationships exist between teachers and administrators, teacher turnover is reduced, and the teacher's commitment to the school is stronger, especially at high-poverty schools. When these relationships exist, they also have an enormous positive impact on teacher retention. Collaborative school relationships also improve teachers' perceptions of the working conditions at the school site (Rubinstein & McCarthy, 2016).

When teachers experience stress from all actors in the school system – students, parents, administrators, and even other teachers – it must be addressed. Attending to teachers' relationships with administrators and families can go a long way to healing the trauma experienced (Adams et al., 2018). However, it will require teachers and administrators to remember that they are on the same team and that working together for the "school's good" is better for everyone.

> **Pause and Reflect:** *Describe your relationship with your administrator. In what ways can it be improved?*
>
> **Act:** *Share an appreciation with a colleague, administrator, student, or parent.*

Seed 4 – Teach with Compassion

Compassion asks that we remain steadfast and engaged even while every fiber of our being wishes to be somewhere else, away from the pain in front of us (Feldman, 2005). In this engagement, we can let go of expectations, demands, and insistence that things should be different and learn to accept what it is (Feldman, 2005). And then, just maybe, with intention, we can ease the suffering of our students and teachers and create a life-affirming school environment for everyone (Feldman, 2005; Quartz et al., 2003). However, remaining compassionate is difficult to do when stressed. Adams et al. (2018) argue that our school system and the actors within it must work to decrease the stress of students, parents, and staff. This can be done by attending to "the hierarchy of basic needs that influence a person's ability and motivation to succeed" (p. 17). If we can reduce the stress students and teachers experience by attending to basic needs we can "develop competence, confidence, and compassion" (p. 20) in our school's climate and working conditions. Doing so will also unleash "critical thinking and creativity" (p. 20) in students as well as school site staff that is desperately needed. Essentially, meeting the needs of students, parents, and staff where they are can create a socially and emotionally safe school environment where compassion and supportive action can flourish (Adams et al., 2018). Addressing compassion fatigue is one basic need that we can attend to for teachers and, by proxy, their students.

The visible disparities experienced by urban students are taking their toll on teachers. Yet, teachers still have a job to do. The obligation and duty to ensure students are learning the curriculum, which is always foremost in the teacher's mind, and they feel guilty when the obligation is not met. This guilt can be compounded by teachers' struggle with their belief that it is easier to have compassion for students who are "easier to handle" than others. Often, the students are perceived to be so challenging that it can inhibit the teacher's desire to want to engage with them, let alone teach them. What's more, these perceptions of urban students, and dare I say all students, factor into the teacher's perceptions of the school's climate – sometimes for the worse.

Feldman's (2005) notion of compassion allows teachers to put themselves in the metaphorical shoes of the students, notice what is occurring, and notice what needs they have that need to be met. However, as a system, we have trained teachers to focus mainly on the intellectual needs of students (Noddings, 2013). That is to teach the academic subject, not the human subject sitting before them. We are training teachers to miss the support and care the student needs in addition to the intellectual stimulation. Approaching education training this way ensures that we are only ever addressing a part of the child, not the whole child (Noddings, 2013). In this way, as a system, we are also only addressing a part of the teacher, not the whole teacher.

Noddings (2013) argues that "the primary aim of every educational institution and of every educational effort must be the maintenance and enhancement of caring" (p. 172). Given that caring is central to compassion, Noddings advocates a compassionate approach to education (Figley, 1995, 2002; Wolpow et al., 2009). This is an approach that recognizes that "teachers are, with students, the heart of the educational process" and thus endeavors to enhance both the self-care of teachers and their capacity to care for students (p. 197). My research shows that teachers are experiencing compassion fatigue, thus compounding the need to shift how we approach preservice training, professional development, and support of teachers so that compassion-centered education becomes the ideal.

> **Pause and Reflect:** *How do you express compassion for students in your classroom? Does this expression shift when dealing with students you perceive to be challenging? If so, how?*
>
> **Act:** *Reflect on your most challenging student, then list your top five Gratitudes for that student. Repeat.*

One Final Thing

I asked to share something with you at the beginning of this book. I wanted to tell you about a pressing issue that should be a significant concern for all teachers at urban schools and the school system charged with retaining teachers – compassion fatigue. Now, I'd like to ask you one more thing. Will you share what you learned in this book with other teachers? Other educators? Encourage them to get a copy of the book and discuss their reactions with you. Watch the TEDx Talk – https://www.youtube.com/watch?v=-Cmc-5sU5L4 – and then share it with colleagues. Host a book club with this as the book of the month. My goal has always been to have compassion fatigue in teachers seen as a serious enough problem to address with governmental action. Until that day comes, we will have to act ourselves. I love school, and teachers are a big part of that. I want the best for you because I know you want the best for students.

> Please take care of yourself.
> Please take care of each other.
> Share!
> You are worth it.
> You matter. Yesterday, today, tomorrow, and always.
> **Thank you for your service.**

 Connect the Thoughts

1. What surprising or significant knowledge did you gain from this chapter?
2. Which seed most resonates with you? Why?
3. How might you share the information you have learned in this chapter with others? This book?

References

Adams, J., Caposey, P. J., & Isiah, R. (2018). *# FULLYCHARGED: 140 Battery charging Maslow and Bloom strategies for students, parents, and staff.* Montery, CA: Healthy Learning.

Banaji, M. R., & Greenwald, A. G. (2016). *Blindspot : Hidden biases of good people: pbk.* New York: Bantam Books.

California Department of Education. (2017). *School conditions and climate work group recommendation framework.* Retrieved February 19, 2024, from https://www.cde.ca.gov/be/pn/im/documents/memo-ocd-oct17item01a1.pdf

Collie, R. J., Shapka, J. D., & Perry, N. E. (2012). School climate and social-emotional learning: Predicting teacher stress, job satisfaction, and teaching efficacy. *Journal of Educational Psychology*, *104*(4), 1189.

Feldman, C. (2005). *Compassion: Listening to the cries of the world.* Berkeley, CA: Rodmell Press.

Figley, C. R. (2002) *Treating compassion fatigue (Brunner-Routledge Psychosocial Stress)* (Kindle Edition). New York: Taylor and Francis.

Figley, C. R. (1995). Compassion fatigue as secondary traumatic stress disorder: An overview. In C. R. Figley (ed.), *Compassion fatigue: Coping with secondary traumatic stress disorder in those who treat the traumatized* (Psychosocial Stress Series) (Kindle Edition) (Vol. 1, pp. 1–18). New York: Taylor and Francis.

Figley, C. R. (2002). Compassion fatigue: Psychotherapists' chronic lack of selfcare. *Journal of Clinical Psychology*, *58*(11), 1433–1441.

Harris, N. B. (2018). *The deepest well: Healing the long-term effects of childhood trauma and adversity* (Kindle). New York: Harper Collins.

National Center for Education Statistics [NCES]. (2022, March). *Number of students receiving selected disciplinary actions in public elementary and secondary schools, by type of disciplinary action, disability status, sex, and race/ethnicity: 2017–18*. Retrieved June 20, 2024, from https://nces.ed.gov/programs/digest/d22/tables/dt22_233.27.asp?current=yes

Noddings, N. (2013). *Caring: A relational approach to ethics and moral education*. Berkeley: University of California Press (Kindle Edition).

Ollison, J. (2019). *Improving teacher retention by addressing teachers' compassion fatigue.* Scholarly Commons. Retrieved February 3, 2024, from https://scholarlycommons.pacific.edu/uop_etds/3602/

Quartz, K. H., Olsen, B., & Duncan-Andrade, J. (2003). *The fragility of urban teaching: A longitudinal study of career development and activism*. UCLA's Institute for Democracy, Education, & Access.

Rubinstein, S. A., & McCarthy, J. E. (2016). Union–management partnerships, teacher collaboration, and student performance. *ILR Review*, *69*(5), 1114–1132. https://doi.org/10.1177/0019793916660508

Tatum, B. (1992). Talking about race, learning about racism: The application of racial identity development theory in the classroom. *Harvard Educational Review*, *62*(1), 1–25.

Wolpow, R., Johnson, M. M., Hertel, R., & Kincaid, S. O. (2009). *The heart of learning and teaching: Compassion, resiliency, and academic success*. Office of Superintendent of Public Instruction (OSPI) Compassionate Schools. Retrieved June 19, 2024, from https://www.k12.wa.us/CompassionateSchools/pubdocs/TheHeartofLearningandTeaching.pdf

Wood, J. L, Harris III, F., & Howard, T. C. (2018). *The capitol of suspensions: Examining the racial exclusion of Black males in Sacramento County*. San Diego: CA Community College Equity Assessment Lab.

Xu, K., Nosek, B. A., Greenwald, A.G., & Lofaro, N. (2018, February 15). Datasets & codebooks. Retrieved from June 19, 2024, https://osf.io/gwofk/

Youth - Mental Health First aid. (2023, November 15). Mental health first aid. Retrieved June 19, 2024, from https://www.mentalhealthfirstaid.org/population-focused-modules/youth/

For Product Safety Concerns and Information please contact our EU
representative GPSR@taylorandfrancis.com
Taylor & Francis Verlag GmbH, Kaufingerstraße 24, 80331 München, Germany

www.ingramcontent.com/pod-product-compliance
Lightning Source LLC
Chambersburg PA
CBHW070739230426
43669CB00014B/2509